SAINT THOMAS AQUINAS

IMMORTALS OF PHILOSOPHY AND RELIGION

SAINT THOMAS AQUINAS

THE ANGELIC DOCTOR

by

Norman Pittenger, S.T.D.

Franklin Watts, Inc.
575 Lexington Avenue
New York, N.Y. 10022

Also by the author:

THE LIFE OF JESUS CHRIST
THE LIFE OF SAINT PAUL
MARTIN LUTHER

Cover photograph courtesy
The New York Public Library

70-4381

CONTENTS

PREFACE

I should like to thank my friends who have helped me in writing this book. Above all, I am grateful to my associates at Saint Edmund's House in Cambridge, a Roman Catholic house of studies attached to the university, which some years ago did me the honor of asking me, a non-Roman Catholic, to become a dining member of the House. The Very Reverend Canon G. D. Sweeney, the Master, and the Reverend J. Derek Holmes, the Dean, have been most generous and kind; and other members of the House have been ready to answer my occasional questions with great courtesy. If this book, whose subject is the greatest of those thinkers to whom the Roman Catholic Church pays respect, introduces others to the man and his place in Western thought, I shall be happy; and perhaps I may offer it to Saint Edmund's as a token of my gratitude.

Norman Pittenger

King's College
Cambridge, England

vii

SAINT THOMAS AQUINAS

The world and travels of Thomas Aquinas,
thirteenth century

1.

"The Angelic Doctor"

"ANGELIC DOCTOR"—that is the title which the Catholic Church has given to Saint Thomas Aquinas, one of the most powerful thinkers in the history of Western civilization. Even those who disagree with what he said acknowledge his greatness and his towering intellect. And anyone who knows the story of his life must also acknowledge his personal qualities, for he was a simple, loving, and lovable man, whose capacity for profound thought was not incompatible with warm humanity.

But why that odd title—Angelic Doctor?

In the golden period of the Middle Ages there were several outstanding Christian thinkers whom the

3

Catholic Church recognized as among its greatest men. They were called doctors, a Latin derivative meaning "learned men." To distinguish among them, it became the custom to call them after some special characteristic of their thought. Of course, this did not happen during their lifetimes. It was when a later generation looked back that the names became appropriate.

Saint Bonaventura, a great thinker who was a member of the Franciscan Order, was called the Seraphic Doctor. His life and writings seemed so inspired by heavenly wisdom that it was as if he had been touched by one of the seraphim, the holy archangels who bring the burning love and wisdom of God to men. This was especially appropriate for a Franciscan, since the founder of their order, Francis of Assisi, was believed to have been visited by a seraph from heaven while in lonely retreat on La Verna, a mountain in central Italy. Saint Thomas' own teacher, Albertus Magnus, was so learned a man, with such an encyclopedic range of knowledge, that he was called the Universal Doctor —that is, he seemed learned in everything. The thinking and writings of the English theologian and philosopher whom we know as Duns Scotus were marked by great subtlety of mind, the drawing of very precise logical distinctions, and an almost razor-sharp way of arguing his points. Thus, he was given the name of Subtle Doctor.

Aquinas was called Angelic Doctor because he wrote so extensively and (as it was thought) so admirably about the angels in whom all Christians then believed. Angels were "pure intelligences, disembodied spirits." They were intermediaries between God and his creation. They served not only to carry out special tasks for which God designated them, but also to fill in the great gap between human beings—defined as souls *with* bodies—and God himself who was sheer spirit, *un*created because He was the creator of all things. The angels were *created* spirits. Originally, they were perfectly good creatures, so the story went; most of them still were such. But a few, headed by Lucifer, their prince, chose their own will and way. Lucifer and his followers "fell" from perfection. They were not "angels of light" but demons, or evil spirits. Thomas wrote much about this whole set of ideas and beliefs, so popular in the Church of his time.

But it is not what Saint Thomas had to say about angels that explains his significance in the history of Western thought. Rather, his importance lies in his extraordinary ability to link together, in a great synthesis, the main affirmations of the Christian faith and the philosophy of the famous Greek thinker Aristotle, whose major writings had been rediscovered about the time of Thomas' birth. When Aristotle's thought first came forcibly to the attention of thinkers in western Europe, it seemed to be in almost total contradiction to everything Christians believed. It was new knowledge for that period. Not only was it new, but it also had the authority that was attached to the writings of

5

the ancient Greeks. Plato and Aristotle, as well as others, were venerated as men of tremendous wisdom. Aristotle's work in observational science was remarkable, and *his* science was taken to be the last word in *all* science.

Thus, there was the traditional Christian faith and there was this "new" science and philosophy. Could they be reconciled? And if they could, in what way? That was the intellectual problem of the High Middle Ages, and every thinker had to face it and seek to resolve it as best he could. Thomas was no exception. He faced the new material in the rediscovered Aristotle, but he was also a devout Christian believer. Most of his mature life was spent in attempting to work out a synthesis of Aristotle's knowledge and the faith that Thomas accepted with his whole heart. His two greatest books, *Summa contra Gentiles* and *Summa Theologica,* as well as almost all his other writings, are concerned with just this issue.

In trying to see why Saint Thomas is so important in the intellectual history of the Western world— Europe, North and South America, as well as other places where European culture has penetrated—we must understand that he was one of those great men who try to view everything whole. Some thinkers interest themselves in one small area of human experience or in one special aspect of the world. They are the people about whom it has been said that they "know more and more about less and less." They are specialists. But Thomas was not that sort of man. He wanted to see how everything fits together. His desire was for a vision of the universe, including man as well as nature; and beyond the universe, or the created world, he desired to see how God, the creator, was related to it.

Two words have often been used to describe Thomas Aquinas: he is called an architechtonic thinker. This complicated-sounding phrase means that he wished to come to some understanding of the interrelationship of things, how everything—from God down to matter— is linked together, and why this should be so. That is a desire which, in our own time, very few thinkers seem to have. Because we know so much about the world, an incredibly larger amount than was possible even to a very learned man in Aquinas' era, we are obliged to spend most of our time studying this or that particular subject. It may be biology or psychology, it may be physics or chemistry, it may be economics or political history. Whatever it is, we give our attention to it. So far as our work in that particular field goes, we can forget what we might call "the big picture." But it was the big picture that fascinated Thomas.

This is why the very few thinkers in the twentieth century who also were fascinated by the big picture were so much attracted to Saint Thomas. Among them was the English-American philosopher Alfred North Whitehead, who died in the 1940's. Another is the famous Frenchman Teilhard de Chardin. These people, and others like them, do not follow the details of Saint Thomas' scheme. On the contrary, they usually depart from it very radically. But the aim Thomas had is also their aim. He is important to them as a man who dared to attempt to study what has been described as "the great chain of being," from dust to divinity.

But Saint Thomas Aquinas was important for still another reason. He was a poet and a hymn-writer. That in itself might not seem to make him matter much. But to a member of the Roman Catholic Church, it can matter a great deal. A Roman Catholic certainly knows two or three very famous hymn-poems which are sung during the service of Benediction and at other times: *O salutaris hostia* ("O, saving victim"), *Tantum ergo* ("Therefore we before Him bending"), *Verbum supernum prodiens* ("The heavenly Word proceeding forth"). Whenever those hymns are sung, Saint Thomas is being remembered, even if his name is not recalled. And when Catholics attend service for Corpus Christi (a yearly celebration of the "Body of Christ" in the Eucharist, or Mass), it is Saint Thomas Aquinas' service which they are using. He wrote the Corpus Christi Office—the special service for that day —at the request of the pope of the time. This fact, in addition to the wide use of his hymns in Roman Catholic and other Christian circles, makes him important, too.

So, Aquinas was a man with a vision of the whole

world, which he wanted to understand so far as the human mind can come to understand it. He was a devout Christian who wrote poems and hymns which have endeared themselves to hundreds of millions of Roman Catholics. But he was also important for a third reason. He was a very bold man, with tremendous courage.

The boldness and courage of Thomas Aquinas did not show themselves in any great exploits in the world. His day-by-day life was not in itself very exciting. After he became a Dominican monk and a teacher, he merely carried on his work and fulfilled his duties, going where he was sent and obeying the orders given to him. Yet his mind was very daring. He believed that it was possible to rethink the Christian faith which he accepted, and to restate it in the terms of the new learning of his day. Believing this, he set out to do it. Consequently, he was often severely criticized, roundly attacked, and on several occasions actually condemned by Church authorities for what he insisted on doing. The fact that not long after his death, those same authorities canonized him—gave him the title of "saint"—and later made his work the officially approved teaching of the Church, does not indicate that he was always looked on with favor during his lifetime. On the contrary, he was regarded as a dangerous thinker. The conservatives of his time considered him a radical and either dismissed his work or attacked it violently.

For a quiet, simple man like Thomas, these reactions were distressing. But he did not let his distress stop him from continuing with his work. He was in the tradition of other great Christian scholars who venture to rethink and restate what others feel to be too sacred to touch in this way. Thus, he is a symbol of a kind of boldness in thought and courage in thinking—qualities not always found in convinced Christian believers.

Although after his death Thomas was called the Angelic Doctor, in his own day he had another nickname. He was known as the Dumb Ox. The reason for that was his large physical frame and his normal silence. In his day, the large and ungainly oxen were used, as they still are in parts of the world, to pull plows, carry heavy objects, and to draw carts carrying produce and equipment.

Thomas was as big in body as in mind. Pictures show him, as somebody has said, as "a kind of walking wine barrel." It is also said that when he was the guest of some very important people, a crescent was cut out of the table so that he could sit comfortably at meals. He himself joked about his corpulence. Perhaps both he and others tended to exaggerate; but there is no doubt that the paintings made shortly after his death show him to be an enormous man, short but extremely heavy.

Many stories have been told about his silence. Sometimes, sitting at dinner, he would not speak throughout the meal. His mind was on something else. As a matter of fact, from what we read, he was thinking most of the time about the problems that fascinated him. In any case, he was a man of few words. And when he was working on some idea or trying to think his way through some intellectual question, he was unable to turn his mind away from it. So he was described as "dumb," silent or taciturn, as we would say.

Last of all, Thomas had two qualities which endeared him to those who knew him well. He had a great capacity for making friends, especially, of course, among those who were with him in the monastery. One of them, Brother Reginald, was very close to him, and has given us much of the story of Thomas' life. During their companionship Thomas evidently, and uncharacteristically, spoke freely about himself and his innermost feelings, hidden from other people.

Thomas' other endearing quality was his quiet humor. For instance, it is said that Saint Thomas, like many other great teachers, was often a little late in arriving in his classroom. He would be engaged in working on an intellectual problem and would lose track of time. Then he would have to hurry through the cloisters to get to his students. One day, during the morning period of absolute silence in the monastery where he was living—silence except for classes such as Thomas conducted—he was hurrying toward his classroom. A statue of Saint Mary spoke to him as he passed by. The statue said, "Thomas, Thomas, late again." Rather than being startled, Thomas, the legend tells

11

us, replied quietly, "This, my Lady, is the hour of silence," and went on his way. There are other tales like this, showing that the great thinker, the angelic doctor, and the dumb ox was a very human person, with a sly sort of humor and a ready wit.

The story of Saint Thomas Aquinas must give an account of his life and a summary of his thought. It is not easy to do the latter, since his thought is profound and has engaged the attention of a great many learned men who have tried to understand and explain it. Yet it is not so complicated as some people have believed. But first we must know of Thomas' early days, as well as something of life and thought in the thirteenth century, when he lived. Only then will it be possible to consider his years of study and the philosophic system he built.

2.

Thomas' Early Years

IF a visitor to Italy travels by automobile from Rome to Naples on the highway that passes the famous monastery Monte Cassino, he will see a sign, a little less than eighty miles from Rome, which indicates a side road to Aquino. If he takes that road and drives less than two miles, he will find himself in the town.

Aquino was a city of the ancient Volsci, one of the early and pre-Roman Italian people; it was the birthplace of the great Latin writer of satire Juvenal. It also possesses the ruins of an old Romanesque church, Santa Maria della Libera. Nearby are more impressive and interesting Roman ruins.

13

But not many tourists bother to visit Aquino. They are too anxious to get to Monte Cassino. The great monastery was destroyed by Allied bombardment during World War II, in the mistaken belief that German troops, perhaps even the German High Command, occupied the place. The monastery was completely rebuilt as soon as the war ended. It contains the tombs of the two noted founders of the Benedictine Order and its women's equivalent, Saints Benedict and Scholastica, and it has a library and archives of extraordinary value.

However, Aquino has a very special interest. Near this town is the Roccasecca, the castle whose name means "dry rock or fortress." Thomas was born there in the year 1226. The name by which he is generally known, Thomas Aquinas—or Thomas of Aquino—is taken from the town near his parents' castle. And so the little place, so infrequently visited, is known to the world through the name of its greatest son.

The surrounding countryside, and especially to the west toward the Tyrrhenian Sea (part of the Mediterranean off western Italy), is in many ways Thomas' country. Not too far away is Monte San Giovanni, where he was imprisoned for a time. The monastery of Monte Cassino itself was where he first went to school. In the nearby town of Maenza, Thomas' niece, the daughter of his brother Philip, made her home, and Thomas often visited her there. Her husband, Annibaldo of Ceccano, was a great benefactor of the not

14

distant monastery of Fossa Nova, where Thomas died on March 7, 1274. He had been taken there from his niece's home, since, as he said, it was better for him as a monk to die in a "religious house."

If the traveler goes on to Naples, after seeing Aquino, he will be in a city where Thomas spent much of his last years, organizing a *studium generale,* or special course of studies, for the young novices of the Dominican Order to which he belonged. There, too, Thomas worked on his *Summa Theologica,* although he left it unfinished. There he composed his last commentaries on the philosophy of Aristotle; and there he preached, in the vernacular Italian of his day, a series of Lenten sermons. Naples, Salerno to the south, and many other towns and cities in the neighborhood are full of reminiscences of the great Christian theologian and philosopher. But Aquino and Fossa Nova are of special importance. Thomas belongs to this part of Italy more than to any other place, although his fame was won during his years in Paris and elsewhere in northern Europe.

The countryside halfway between Rome and Naples is very beautiful. The land is uneven, with many valleys, where even today farmers work hard to make a living, and with hills and ranges of mountains which rise up into the blue Italian sky. Almost everywhere there are ruins of ancient Roman towns, whose stones were used by later residents to build their own houses. The old Roman roads, like the Via Latina and the Via

Appia, traverse the territory. Their modern successors carry most of the traffic between the two great cities. There are castles, like that in which Thomas was born, dominating the valleys. There are fascinating Italian hill towns, each set on its hilltop, each with its towers and its churches, each with houses huddled around the castle or church as if for protection from marauders. The people are friendly and talkative, speaking a quick Italian which the foreigner, if not skilled in that tongue, finds difficult because of the dialect which they use. This part of the Italian peninsula is peculiarly attractive, since here—more perhaps than anywhere else in the land—one has the specially Italian mixture of old and new, classical and romantic, the very soil seeming to be impregnated with history.

Thomas' family had its history, too. His was a princely family; one might almost say a royal one. Of course, he had Italian ancestors, but in those days the continent of Europe was not so divided into separate lands, and there was much going and coming and much intermarriage. There was also German and French blood in Thomas' background. His second cousin was the Emperor Frederick II, known to history as *Stupor Mundi* ("the wonder of the world") because of his brilliance and learning. Thomas' great-uncle was that romantic and strange figure Barbarossa, a sea pirate. On the French side, Thomas had Norman ancestors. The Normans had come from France into the peninsula of Italy and had been especially prominent in the section around Naples, as well as in Sicily. But the main family line was that of the counts of Aquino; Thomas' father was the Count Landulf of Aquino, whose headquarters was the castle on the "dry rock" where Thomas was born.

He was the seventh son in a large family, a quiet boy and always big for his age. One story says that as a very young lad he was already noted for his long silences, broken on occasion by startling questions. One day, he astounded his tutor by asking, out of the blue, "What is God?" We do not know what answer the teacher gave him, but that question provides a clue to the whole of Thomas' life. Throughout his career, as a schoolboy at Monte Cassino, as a young friar, as a student in Cologne, as a teacher and lecturer, as a philosopher and theologian, and as the author of an enormous number of books, everything came back to God—who God is, what he is like, how men may know about him, and how they may know him.

But as a small child, living on a southern Italian hilltop, Thomas was mostly interested in playing with his brothers and sisters. He was oblivious of his historical background and the princely blood in his veins. Someone has said that if Thomas had wished to do so, he might have had placed on his shield the crests of half the kingdoms which then existed in Europe. But family traditions and lineage were not important to him, once he had made his decision about what his vocation in life was to be. This is one of the things that makes him such a fascinating personality.

The Lady Theodora, Thomas' mother, was of a

noble family from Naples. It seems that she died some-where in the 1250's; his father died about 1244. After the count's death, Aimo, the oldest of Thomas' brothers, became the head of the family. He is men-tioned in a papal document of the year 1254 as being faithful to the Holy See, the Roman court where the pope resided. In 1266 Aimo became justiciar of King Charles of Anjou (who controlled Naples and southern Italy) in the island of Sicily. This meant that Aimo was a kind of legal administrator of justice on that island.

Besides Aimo, Thomas had five other brothers, James, Adeuulf, Philip, Landulf, and Reginald. His five sisters were Marotta, Mary, Theodora, Adelasia, and an unnamed girl who died in infancy. The young-est boy, Thomas was also younger than Marotta and Theodora, and perhaps Mary. On the whole it seems to have been a happy family; certainly Lady Theodora was devoted to her children. One of the early writers about Thomas speaks of this devotion, and remarks that she was "a lady whose memory should be held dear by all good men."

In his very early years, Thomas was put in the care of a nurse, who taught him manners and perhaps even the beginning of his letters. But shortly after his fifth birthday, his parents decided that they would send their youngest son to the school for boys at the abbey of Monte Cassino. There he was to be trained "in good morals," as an ancient biographer puts it, and

18

given the advantage of the excellent education which the monastery school provided. This was by no means unusual for boys of noble families. There were no other schools for children to attend—girls would not have gone in any event—and the centers of learning in the Middle Ages were the religious houses.

Very little is known of Thomas' days at Monte Cassino, although there is evidence that he proved to be a studious child. In the account of his life by Bernard Gui, written not many decades after Thomas' death, it is said that the boy "was continually to be seen pondering over the books which contained the little exercises and lessons suited to his age." He was remembered as "a quiet boy with an unusually mature bearing" and he "said little. but thought much, being rather silent and serious and evidently much given to prayer."

Even though Gui says that Thomas did not much participate in "the childish occupations of the other noble lads who were his companions in the school," it is evident that he was sufficiently well liked both by the other boys and by the teachers and the responsible authorities of the monastery school. The authorities believed that "the future held much in store for Thomas," and they were anxious to promote his further study.

But the monastery school could hardly provide adequate instruction for a boy so acute intellectually as Thomas. The Lady Theodora, who remained at

Roccasecca, the family castle, while her husband went off on his various official duties, was delighted to receive the excellent reports about the rapid progress her son was making in the school. Therefore, she was prepared to agree to a suggestion made by the abbot at Monte Cassino. The abbot, said to have been Landulf Sinibadio and a relation of the Aquino family, wanted the boy to receive further academic training at the University of Naples. Thomas was then about fourteen.

The University of Naples had been founded a few years before, in 1224. It was beginning to rival the great university at Bologna, although it did not achieve the fame of that older place of study. Although it may seem unusual today to think of a fourteen-year-old boy going to a university, this was common in the Middle Ages. There were probably dozens, perhaps hundreds, of youths about Thomas' age studying with him in Naples.

Since Thomas had been sent to the university from the Benedictine monastery of Monte Cassino, he would have been housed in the hostel for Benedictine students in Naples. It was customary for the various religious orders to have such places of residence for young men. They lived in the hostel, where they also had their meals. They received the benefit of association with like-minded students and developed a common life. The situation was very much like that which still prevails in the ancient English universities of Oxford and Cambridge, where students live and eat together in the particular college to which they belong. They make friends among fellow members of the college, and have a certain amount of supervision from the older, or senior, residents who teach in the university but also belong to this or that particular college. Lectures and all teaching are carried out through the university, however, although some of the instruction of a more personal nature might also be given in the college, or, in Thomas' case, in the hostel.

As a university undergraduate Thomas continued to exhibit a lively intelligence. He studied grammar and logic with a man called Master Martin. Later he studied natural science with a lecturer named Master Peter (who came from Ireland to Naples to join the teaching staff—an illustration of the way in which even in those times in the academic world there was a good deal of travel and exchange of teachers between countries). Gui says that the young Thomas showed "depth and subtlety of mind," and stood high among those who belonged to his year at the university.

Thomas remained at Naples until 1244. A year earlier he had become a member of the Order of Preachers, the Dominican preaching brotherhood. This decision, which was entirely his own, set the seal upon his life. From that point on, despite many difficulties, he was a devoted member of the order. His determination to enter that society seems to have been, to some degree, for the purpose of assisting in the development

21

of a sound intellectual basis for the Christian faith. For throughout his years in Naples, as in his earlier period at the monastery, his religious life and convictions had continued strong. Here was a way in which he could combine a life devoted specifically to religious practices with his growing intellectual curiosity and his urgent desire to bring to the Church the services of what—as he must have known—were intellectual qualities of a high order.

Thomas was encouraged in his resolve by a celebrated Dominican friar, John of San Giuliano, who was in Naples at the time and who talked with the young man about his vocation. The boy was only eighteen when his decision was made, an early age for reception into the order. The ceremony of reception included the "clothing" of the candidate in the habit of the order. This was done by Thomas Agni of Lentini, at that time prior of the Dominican house in Naples, later bishop of Cosenza in southern Italy, and afterward patriarch of the Latin communion in Jerusalem. Thomas Agni was a distinguished priest and a dutiful Dominican. His "clothing" of Aquinas is an indication of the high esteem that Agni had for the new brother.

There has been much discussion about Thomas' admission to the Dominicans at such an early age. If he was, indeed, about eighteen, his admission was unusual but not unique. However, some historians have thought that he was only fifteen or sixteen at the time.

22

This would have meant a strange violation of the rules. Furthermore, there is a problem about his parents' consent. If he were younger than eighteen, parental consent would have been required. But Thomas' father disapproved of the whole idea. The count wanted his youngest son to continue at Monte Cassino, and become a regular member of the Benedictine Order. Doubtless, the older Aquino, proud of his family connections with that famous and ancient religious house, had plans for Thomas to become the abbot there or in some similar house.

All in all, there seems no reason to doubt the majority opinion that Thomas was, in fact, eighteen, or nearly so. He became a member of the Roman province of the order, with his permanent home at the Dominican priory in Naples. The priory had been established in 1231, and two years later, when the founder of the order, Saint Dominic, was canonized by the Church, the priory in Naples was dedicated to him.

When Thomas' mother heard the news, she was gratified, because she had always thought that her son was destined for the religious life. To be a member of the Dominicans would be, she felt, an excellent way of realizing this vocation. But the count remained unhappy. And soon, Lady Theodora changed her mind, too. When she went to Naples hoping to see Thomas, she found that he had been sent to the city of Rome. The explanation is simple. When the friars in Naples heard that Lady Theodora was to visit there, they assumed that she might wish to persuade Thomas to give up his membership in their order. Not finding Thomas in Naples, she went to Rome. Once again he was gone, for he had been "put on the road north to Tuscany," the region of Florence. We do not know why this was done.

In any event, his mother was angry. She sent a message to Roccasecca, asking her other sons to stop their brother on the way north, if they were able to do so, and to bring him home by force, if no other method proved effective. There is good reason to think that her husband persuaded her to do this. The message to her sons went from Roccasecca to the town of Acquapendente, north of Rome on the route to Florence. The sons were there with the court of the Emperor Frederick, attached to the emperor's entourage. Somehow the message traveled very swiftly, for it reached the brothers in time for them to carry out their mother's directions.

Acquapendente is a little to the north of Lake Bolsena. It is near the Via Cassia, then the main road from Rome to the upper part of Italy. Therefore, it was easy to apprehend Thomas. The brothers swooped down on the Via Cassia and intercepted the little party of Dominicans resting at a roadside spring. When the armed Aquino brothers appeared, mounted on horses and accompanied by their men-at-arms, no resistance was possible. The young friar refused for a moment, but it was hopeless. He was placed on a horse and car-

24

ried off to the south—far beyond Rome itself. At first he was held in the castle of Monte San Giovanni, which is near Frosinone. Later, during May, 1244, he was transferred to the family castle at Roccasecca. This was the year of his father's death.

The full details of Thomas' confinement at the fortress castle of Monte San Giovanni are not known. However, his brothers tried to persuade him to give up his vocation to become a preaching friar of the Dominican Order. But Thomas was adamant. He had decided on his course and he would not swerve from it. Then his brothers decided upon another scheme, one that today we would call "a dirty trick." They brought into the castle a woman of loose morals who attempted to seduce Thomas. In this way, the brothers thought that they could force the order itself to dismiss Thomas from membership. But they were disappointed in their efforts. When Thomas saw the woman, he jumped from his chair, seized a burning faggot from the fireplace, and forced her to leave. It is one of the few times when Thomas seems to have been really angered.

The Dominican Order was outraged at what had happened. Thomas had been with some of them as they took the Via Appia, along the seacoast from Naples to Rome, and proceeded north toward Tuscany. In Rome they had lodged briefly at Santa Sabina, given to Saint Dominic by Pope Honorius III in 1220, to serve as a residence for the order in that city. Then they had started their northward journey—the destination seems to have been Bologna, where there was to be a general chapter (a sort of congress) of the order. It appears that in the company was the head of the Dominicans himself, John of Wildeshausen, the Master General, who was of German origin. To find themselves waylaid by a group of ruffians, as they regarded Thomas' brothers, and to have one of their number carried away against his wishes, seemed to them a shocking business. Hence, they made an appeal to Pope Innocent IV, who was in Tuscany at the time.

The pope was concerned, too, and took up the matter with the Holy Roman Emperor, who was Frederick. The pope asked for an investigation of the incident, which he felt to be criminal, and for the restoration of Thomas to the Dominicans, along with due punishment for the men who had kidnapped their brother. The whole situation was complicated by the fact that at the moment the Emperor Frederick was still under sentence of excommunication, because of his opposition to papal activities in central Italy. Indeed, he had allied himself with some of the enemies of the papal cause. But for strategic reasons, if for no others, Frederick responded favorably to the pope's request. He asked that there be an investigation, although he did not order the young friar's immediate release from confinement at Monte San Giovanni, and later at Roccasecca, but family rights might have been involved there.

The emperor's agreement to have an inquiry seems

to have satisfied the Dominicans, especially because they were getting themselves mixed up in a disagreement at a very high level, between pope and emperor. Any pressing of the issue might very likely have worsened the Church-Empire situation which, thanks to the emperor's promise of investigation, seemed to have been improved. So Thomas was left, for the time, in his brothers' custody. His confinement lasted for two years, during which the young man continued his private study, and found that his own inner spiritual life was deepened by his trials.

During his months in confinement, Thomas was visited occasionally by the Dominican friar John of San Giuliano. In order to make these visits, John was obliged to resort to subterfuge. Friar John not only wished to give spiritual comfort to the young friar, nineteen at the time, but one account says that he also brought Thomas changes of clothing, for which no provision had been made during his imprisonment. John would make his visit wearing two of the habits proper to the order. He would take one off and give it to Thomas, it is said, and wear the old habit out of the fortress-castle.

One record mentions some of the books that Thomas studied during the two years he was confined. He read the Bible with great care. He also read the famous volume of *Sentences* by Peter Lombard. Some of the few available writings of Aristotle were probably on his list of books to study; mention is made of the

Greek philosopher's *Organon*. Of course, Thomas also had his Breviary—the book of daily services which monks and nuns used—and he observed, so far as it was possible, "all the laws of the Order," as one of the early biographers states. That means that he read the "hours," or special parts of the Breviary appointed to be said during the day; attended the mass which would naturally have been said in the chapels both at Monte San Giovanni and in his own home at Roccasecca; and followed the rules about fasting and other regular practices of the Dominican Order.

His time spent in study was useful in later years, for it had not only given him a further grounding in the ordinary academic training of the time, but it also developed helpful habits which he never lost. He learned to concentrate on his reading. He also learned to read with more speed than seems to have been common at the time, while also retaining what he read. It would be a mistake, of course, to assume that during those years Thomas was chained in a dungeon or subjected to physical privations or suffering. The confinement meant simply that he must remain within the precincts of the castle.

After Thomas arrived under guard at Roccasecca, he was able, despite his confinement, to do something which he had always wanted to do. He could teach. And so he began to instruct his sisters in the Christian faith. One of them, Marotta, was so influenced by her brother that she decided to enter a religious order. Soon she entered the Benedictine convent for women at Capua. In 1252, not much more than seven years after her admission, she was elected the abbess of that convent, which was confirmed by Pope Innocent IV in 1254. Marotta died five or six years later.

One interesting story says that while he was a prisoner, Thomas wrote some poetry for the first time. Although he later composed Latin verses for a religious service, his first poetry seems to have been written in Italian. The one poem which has been preserved is a sonnet. It is somewhat stilted and stiff, even in the Italian original, showing not much imagination, but vigorous and intense in spirit. One commentator has said that "It is the sort of poem which might have been written by a chaste and intelligent student whose later development would not be in the field of poetry." Certainly young Thomas was just that sort of person. On the other hand, the diction of the poem is much like the then vernacular verse of the so-called Sicilian school. Since Thomas had connections of this sort, through his family, it is likely that he had read and enjoyed some of these other bits of poetry, which were known in Naples and probably also to his family at Roccasecca.

The following is a prose translation of Thomas' sonnet:

A man has virtue just so far as he has understanding; and he is a worthy person to the degree that he is virtuous. The good at which he aims, as he nobly rejoices in everything

29

that has an excellent intention, is the very good that he also comes to possess. And his noble joy causes a beautiful desire in his heart, a desire which shines the more beautifully because it reflects, as with the light, the likeness that exists between his knowledge and his excellent pleasure in thought.

Whoever, therefore, would judge whether a man is worthy of honor and of praise must consider what that man's heart truly desires. All men strive for happiness; but that man can most expect to gain the crown who does his work, whatever it may be, for the sake of the true honor (which is to serve the excellent and the good).

The poem is very intellectual, very abstract, and without images or symbols, save for the "reflection" line. In English it sounds even more academic and stilted than in the Italian. Why did Thomas write it? One possibility is that he was speaking of himself, trying to explain that he was seeking what he regarded as excellent and good—that is, membership in the Dominicans—and must be judged by that standard, rather than by some artificial standard, such as supposed family position or privilege. One thing, however, is clear. Thomas had a facility for Italian rhythm and rhyme, because despite the rather stilted language he finds again and again just the right cadence and the right rhyming word in his sonnet. Reading the sonnet aloud in its original gives an impression of genuine beauty of language, despite the academic subject and the stiffness of style.

In the summer of 1245, Thomas got away from his family prison. Biographer Gui writes that "his mother, realizing . . . that to resist her son any longer would be to resist providence, cunningly gave orders that the guard was to be relaxed so that it would be possible for Thomas to escape, which he did by the use of a rope let down from the window of his room." There is no reason to doubt the accuracy of the story, although other reports simply say that "Thomas was permitted to leave Roccasecca."

Thomas went at once to Naples, where again he made his home in the Dominican house. For a short period he remained in the city, taking up once again —and with no interference from his family—his regular life in the order. The senior staff of the Dominican house found that Thomas had indeed profited from the reading which he had done during his confinement. Gui says that he showed himself "so advanced in his studies that it was as if he had passed through a long period of study in the Schools"—the reference is to the further training which a university student would have obtained in the academic environment of the lecture room and the disputation sessions. In fact, his superiors were so pleased at his progress that they decided to send him to Paris for further study, and later to Cologne, where the famous Albertus Magnus directed a school of theology and philosophy.

Thomas accompanied the then Master General John, who had an engagement in Paris in 1246. This journey was not made overland and entirely on foot, as was commonly the case for friars, and as we know (from other material) was Thomas' usual way of travel. Instead, the group took the sea route to France; there was a regular service between Naples and southern France. We know that Thomas sailed to France because one of his early biographers says that once he had experienced the perils of a storm at sea. Although there is no information for this particular journey, the records make clear that on every other trip Thomas went by foot. Therefore, it is logical to presume that *this* was the sea journey where he experienced a storm. A good deal of the sequence of Thomas' life must be pieced together in this fashion. This is not surprising, however, for during the actual occurrence of the events Thomas was not an important person and there was no reason to keep a careful record of his every movement.

In Paris, Thomas was attached to the priory school of Saint Jacques, one of the intellectual centers of the Dominican Order. At that time, Saint Jacques was the only *studium generale,* an international school maintained by the Dominicans. To their great pride, it attracted brilliant scholars from all over the world. Albertus Magnus was there from 1245 to 1248. Therefore, it was in Paris, rather than in Cologne, that Thomas Aquinas met the man who was most influential in his life and who opened to him the subject to which he would devote the remainder of his days.

Albertus, the Universal Doctor, who seemed to know everything there was to be known and who yet preserved a firm religious faith, was especially interested in the reconciliation of philosophy with theology. He had read the newly discovered works of Aristotle, and he respected the great Greek thinker for his honesty, logical clarity, and knowledge. At the same time, Albertus realized that it was necessary for Christian scholars to find ways in which what Aristotle said could be fitted into the Christian faith. Otherwise, he believed, learned people would regard the Christian position as contradictory to sound thought and reasoning. Albertus was sure that this need not happen, for all truth comes from a single source—God who *is* "the Truth"—and there cannot be any ultimate contradiction between what is true in thought and what is true in faith. This conviction communicated itself to his young student Thomas, who determined to give his time and effort to developing such a way of thinking and believing, in harmonious concord.

Albertus Magnus had been born in Lauingen in Swabia, a part of what is now Germany, probably in 1200. Therefore, he was about twenty-five years older than Thomas. He died in 1280, honored still as one of the greatest scholars of the century, although his student, who died a few years before, had also achieved international fame. Albertus studied in Padua in northern Italy, not far from Venice, and while there he entered the Dominican Order. He returned to Germany to teach for a short time, but was soon called to

Paris where he held one of the Dominican chairs of theology before going to Cologne in 1248. From then until 1254, he was head of the new *studium* in Cologne, with Thomas Aquinas as his most brilliant and promising pupil. In 1254 Albertus was chosen to be "provincial" of the Dominicans for all of Germany, supervising the work of the order in that land. He was responsible for the reorganization of the program of studies for his order, which was effected in 1259. The following year he was made bishop of Ratisbon in Germany, against his own wish and that of Humbert of Romanus, who was then Master General of the Dominicans. Fortunately, Albertus was able to resign in 1262. A few years later he returned to Cologne, again to teach in the *studium*. He was in attendance at the Council of Lyons in 1274, the year of Thomas' death.

When Thomas died, his theological opinions and his philosophical use of Aristotle were under considerable attack. It is therefore interesting, and a touching tribute to an old man's respect for a much younger student, that Albertus went to Paris in 1276 to defend Thomas' name and work. University theologians were entirely opposed to the way in which Thomas had used Aristotle for Christian purposes. Albertus' efforts were not entirely successful, however, since, in 1277, Bishop Tempier of Paris was able to include some of Thomas' positions in his official condemnation of "false theological ideas." Albertus returned to Cologne, where he died on November 15, 1280. In 1931, Pope Pius XI canonized him as a saint.

This was the teacher who would inspire young Thomas Aquinas. And Albertus saw before him a brilliant student, a member of a noble family, who had been a promising boy and youth. Thomas was a young man of spiritual insight and deep devotion, and a very human person who was liked by his associates. He was also a young man with a mind of his own.

Thomas had his own convictions, born from his years of study and thought, and these convictions were brought into sharp focus when he met and studied under Albertus Magnus. He saw that his vocation in life was to work out, so far as he could, a way in which the secular wisdom newly discovered in the writings of Aristotle might be brought into the service of the Christian faith. Having come to this position, he showed once again the same tenacity of purpose as that which had led him to resist all persuasion from his family. He was a man of genuine courage, especially in the intellectual sphere. In setting himself the task of reconciling secular thought and Christian faith, he was engaging in a risky business, not only because of the opposition of many leaders in the Church but also because he faced the possibility that his proposed reconciliation might fail, to the damage of the faith which he so devoutly held. Intellectual courage is courage of the highest order, although many do not recognize this. Thomas had it, and he demonstrated it by the boldness with which he familiarized himself with a kind of thinking that was regarded by many as highly dangerous.

3.

Life and Thought in the
Thirteenth Century

THE thirteenth century has been called "the golden period of the Middle Ages." It was the time of a great flowering of art, the building of some of the most beautiful of cathedrals and other pieces of Gothic architecture, the development of the universities which had been established in the preceding century, and the writing of some of the most important books in the history of Western thought. It was also "the age of faith," when the whole of Europe, including the British Isles, was part of one religious community. Everyone living in those lands was a member of the Catholic Church—with greater or less personal devotion—but, nevertheless, accepting that one universal religious body as the representative of the Christian religion in the world.

There was not complete uniformity, however, for there were many different ways of approaching and understanding the common faith, differing not only from country to country but from city to city. In intellectual circles, the major interest was in the attempt to find ways in which that accepted faith could be put into words that made sense at the time. It was a period of very great intellectual activity. But it was also an age when only a few people could afford to take the leisure time for thinking, since there was also much conflict and dispute in political matters. And for the ordinary man or woman, whatever his place in the regimented social structure, it was a time of hard work and sometimes of genuine deprivation and want. The peasants who farmed the lands of their lords and the workmen in the shops and guilds had neither the education nor the interest to occupy themselves in intellectual pursuits. They had to eke out a living, and that was no easy matter.

When we think of Europe today, we have a picture of a number of countries with clearly defined boundaries, each under its own government. But in Thomas' time this was not the case. A sense of national identity had not yet developed. People were much more the citizens of this or that city, or area under a king, duke, or prince. They were often passionately loyal, but their loyalty was to their immediate surrounding homeland.

Thus, in Italy, for instance, there was loyalty to a city such as Florence or Siena or Naples, but there was also rivalry with, and sometimes great jealousy of, other nearby cities. The residents were Florentines, Sienese, or Neapolitans; they were not properly *Italians* as yet. Actually, the sense of being a nation did not really emerge in Italy until the nineteenth century.

Elsewhere, national feeling appeared in the sixteenth and seventeenth centuries, as in Germany during the days of Martin Luther. In England, this development took place a century or so earlier. But England was part of an island, fairly small and compact, and even then Scotland still remained Scotland, an independent and not much united land, because the various local clans claimed the loyalty of the people.

Of course, there was what was called "the Holy Roman Empire," which was supposed to include almost all of western Europe (from Poland to the Pyrenees, at least, and excluding the British Isles and Scandinavia). But the "empire" was more a theory than a reality. Claimed to be the successor of the old Roman Empire of pagan days, it had been Christianized in the time of Constantine in the fourth century, and its great ideal ruler was Charlemagne, who had been crowned as emperor at the turn of the ninth century. But even Charlemagne had not actually been in control of all that went under the name of the Holy Roman Empire, and after his death, the territories split up under different rulers.

The social pattern of life at the time was stratified. At the top were the rulers of cities, or small states including several cities and the surrounding countryside. Each had its court, to which belonged the "ministers of state" who looked after the affairs of the ruler. If one of the cities was called a republic, it did not mean what we mean by the term today. It indicated only that the leading businessmen—perhaps, the rich families and those of aristocratic lineage—chose a council or senate to act as a final governing body, appointing some important man to be the mayor or the *doge* (duke) or president. The mass of the population was not consulted and had no share in government.

Next came the class of petty magnates, each with his own land and usually with his own castle dominating the territory which he owned and controlled. So it was with Thomas' own father. Count Landulf of Aquino possessed the castle known as Dry Rock, standing on the peak of a crag which overlooked miles of rolling countryside, much of it farmed but some of it still fairly wild and untamed woods and rock.

A complicating factor in the pattern of society was the presence of large "religious houses," which also owned and controlled land. In all the great places, whether secular like that of Aquino, or religious like the monasteries, lived another class of people. These included knights and their ladies. The knights were drawn from what we might describe as the upper-middle class, or perhaps from the younger sons of

39

princely families. They were always associated with one of the courts, serving the ruler as trained soldier-officers, defending him and his lands from attack or damage, fighting for him if he took it into his head to engage in marauding raids on some neighboring princelet, and otherwise ornamenting his court with their presence. Modern man tends to have altogether too romantic a picture of the knights of the Middle Ages. They were not all Sir Galahads, by any means. But they did follow certain rules of chivalry, and they were a class of fairly respectable and responsible men, just as their ladies were women of position and good manners.

The next class of society was composed of the rich merchants and traders who lived in the cities and engaged in business, either independently or in groups. Several centuries later, during the days of the Reformation, such men became very prominent in the affairs of their cities or states. But in the time of Saint Thomas, they had not yet acquired such importance. They might try, and succeed at, buying their way into the knightly rank. But insofar as they were engaged "in trade" they tended to be somewhat looked down upon, although their presence and their activity were necessary for the maintenance of society, since they provided the articles that everyone above the rank of peasant needed.

In each city there were associations of trained artisans, organized for the most part in guilds, which existed to protect their interests, establish a just price for their wares, and assure that young assistants were properly trained to do the work and to achieve recognition after serving long years in apprenticeships. The guilds often became very rich, since they could pretty well control the commodities which they produced and see to it that they got good prices for what they made and sold. Goldsmiths, coppersmiths, makers of fine (and not so fine) linens, spice merchants, sellers of produce brought in from the countryside—these were some of the people who were in the class of trained artisans, salesmen, shopkeepers, and manufacturers of wares.

Finally, at the bottom of the social scale were the men and women who worked on the land or in the mines or on the ships—wherever there was hard manual labor to be done. These serfs were tied to the land on which they lived; they belonged, in the most literal sense, to the landowners. They had their rights, of course, and they were also protected, at least in law if not always in fact, from a landowner's misuse and bad treatment. But they were usually desperately poor, living in what amounted to hovels, often with large families. They worked hard; they had to struggle to get what little they had to live on; they were completely uneducated, although now and then a peasant boy would manage to attract some magnate or knight or prince, who would take him into his home and bring him up to better things. But this was very much the exceptional case. Furthermore, people remained in their class. A boy of a peasant family himself became a peasant, and a girl married a peasant and became a peasant's wife, ending his or her days in the same status as that which they knew in childhood.

Since the serfs were entirely uneducated, they were generally superstitious. Of course, this was not confined to the serfs, for there was a great deal of superstition in the Middle Ages, even in "the golden period." But the situation was much worse the farther down one went in the social scale. This explains why so many beliefs, to us quite absurd, could flourish about evil spirits, demon possession, charms, and the like.

Actually, no matter at what level of society, life was not easy in the thirteenth century. Just as we look at knighthood too romantically, so we also have overly romantic ideas of what life was like in a castle, such as that in which Thomas was born. Castles were really rather terrible places. A look at one of them almost anywhere in Europe would prove it to be fairly typical of all castles.

The castle was perched on a hilltop, access to it possible only by a fairly steep road which curved around the slope from the valley beneath. Of course, it might just as well have been in fairly flat country, in which case a moat would have surrounded it, with draw-bridges that could be pulled up to shut out intruders. But, in the case of a hilltop castle, any visitor who was not welcome could be taken care of satisfactorily by dropping heavy stones down on him from the fortified walls. At the front of the castle was a great gateway, with thick doors of wood which could be kept closed against intruders.

The welcome visitor entered through the gateway and found himself in a not very large central court. It was paved with cobblestones, and around the sides were several doors leading to various rooms in the castle. The rooms were fairly large if they were intended for common use—the hall for dining or meetings with other magnates or counts, for example, was of good size. Above the halls, however, the rooms were very small. These were the bedrooms, the tiring-, or dressing-, rooms, and the various offices used by the family of the prince or by his servants.

Inside, the walls were hung with tapestries, to give some protection from the cold. The windows were tiny slits in the wall, covered by heavy curtains to keep out wind and rain. Many of the rooms contained small fireplaces or braziers to make them endurable in winter. The great halls had enormous fireplaces.

Life in a medieval castle must have been most uncomfortable; certainly better than life in a serf's hovel, but not so pleasant as in the palace of a city magnate or merchant-prince. For one thing, castle sanitary facilities were appallingly primitive. For another, the kitchens and storerooms must have been smelly and disagreeable spots. For a third, privacy must have been hard to come by, since often the sleeping quarters were connected in such a way that a person had to go through one of them to get to another. All in all, Thomas would not have known much about what we would call not only the comforts and conveniences of life, but even the bare necessities for decent living.

However, nobody at that time was conscious of any deprivation. This was the universal way of life, and people could be as happy, or as sad, in those circumstances as we are today in our own situations. And children of families like that of Count Landulf of Aquino could be very happy indeed. They could play in the courtyard, having their own brothers and sisters for companions, as well as the children of the attendant knights and even of the higher-placed servants. Discipline was severe, but in many households the children were loved, well treated, and given a reasonably good education by their parents or tutors. Little girls were not supposed to be scholars, but they learned the manners and customs of "ladies," while boys (as it was thought befitted them) were taught to read and write, if this were possible, and were trained in deportment appropriate to their station in life. As soon as they were old enough, the boys would accompany their fathers (as Thomas did) on some short trips on horseback, seeing something of the world outside the castle and learning how to behave as guests of neighboring dignitaries. Also, there were frequent visitors at a castle, some of them coming from great distances or from foreign lands. Thus, the children often came to know something concerning the great world itself.

As most large castles had a chapel attached, with a resident chaplain, religious instruction and practice were also part of the ordinary way of life. Mass was said daily in the chapel, and there were gala celebrations at the great festivals, perhaps with a bishop making a visitation. These were supplemented by private instruction in the Christian faith, given by the chaplain to the children. In this way, a conscientious family saw that religious duties were fulfilled and that some knowledge, although perhaps not too profound, was provided about the beliefs held by the universal Church.

Whether in a castle or a hovel, in city or country, it was the Church which really held Europe together. The head of the Church was in the city of Rome, the Eternal City that had endured many trials and hardships, including devastation from invaders in earlier centuries and years of bad government which had resulted in poverty and want. But despite this, Rome was the symbol of whatever unity there was in Europe. The pope lived there, as did the *curia,* or court of ecclesiastics, who carried out the pope's will in the Church at large. A large number of pilgrimages and visitations were made to the holy city to see the pope in his residence, which, at that time, was the Lateran Palace.

If the Church was what held Europe together in a great international society, the use of Latin as the common language of all educated persons held the Continent together in another sense. Latin had been the tongue spoken throughout the great Roman Empire several hundred years before. When the empire collapsed, Latin still remained in use. It was not the classical Latin which is taught in school today, for that had faded away during the fourth and fifth centuries. This was "low Latin," as it was called, and as the Italians still like to name their own language (*latino basso*). But classical or "low," it made possible the exchange of ideas throughout the Continent, and it enabled a literate Italian to talk with a literate Englishman, an educated Spaniard to speak with an educated German. Above all, Latin was the official language of the Church itself, not only in its worship but in all its ordinary activities.

As we have indicated, everybody, excepting the Jews who lived in ghettos in the cities of Europe, belonged to the Church. The many Jews who had been forced to leave the Holy Land, or who belonged to the families which for hundreds of years had lived outside Palestine, were accepted but not liked. There was not very much of the appalling anti-Semitism which the world has known in later years, but the general Christian population regarded all Jews as people who had rejected the Savior Christ. Therefore, they tended to look down on them. As a result, the Jewish population was forced to live in special portions of a city. They made their living by trading, moneylending, and small business. But apart from the Jews, the whole world was Christian, at least in name, and in actuality, the Church exercised a very large measure of control even over the lives of the Jews.

Canon law—the rules for conduct and human relations which the Church had set up on the basis of many much older regulations—was vigorously enforced. Disobedience was punished by excommunication or exclusion from sharing in the sacraments, or by other penalties. The Church had its system of courts which paralleled and, in some respects, overruled the civil courts. And at the very summit of the ecclesiastical system was the bishop of Rome and his court of cardinals and dignitaries.

Each smaller area, whether city or state, had its bishop who represented the central papal authority. Such a bishop was usually from a princely family, or at least he was considered as sharing that status. He had immense power, since he, too, could invoke the penalties of excommunication or other punishment for wrongdoing. Then there were monasteries, with abbots or priors in charge. These, too, were men—or female leaders called abbesses or prioresses for the women's orders—of distinction, with much power not only over the membership of their houses but also in the affairs of the territory where they lived. Finally, there were parish priests, usually not very well instructed, who carried on the daily worship of the congregations, and also baptized, performed all marriages,

47

heard confessions, anointed the sick, and buried the dead. Like society at large, the Church was hierarchically ordered, with different grades or classes.

It would be grossly unfair, however, to give the impression that this organizational side of the Church was its most important aspect. Despite the satire found in books such as Chaucer's *Canterbury Tales,* there was a great deal of genuine piety and deep conviction among religious leaders. The bishops and priests, as well as the heads of monasteries and convents, were usually good men and women who performed their duties and were truly concerned for their flocks. In Rome itself the same was true. Therefore, it is not incorrect to speak of the thirteenth century as the age of faith. It would be equally right to speak of it as an age of devotion. There was much concern for charitable works, and at least an effort on the part of untold thousands or millions to live in love and charity with each other, despite the difficult conditions, the poverty, the little or great wars, and all the other problems of the time. And in many families, in all ranks of society, true religion flourished—as it did in Thomas' own family in their castle at Aquino.

The monasteries were an important part of the religious pattern. Some of the orders went back for centuries. The Benedictines, whose great house was at Monte Cassino, were very old. They followed a fairly simple rule of life, combining physical work with intellectual effort, bringing together that sort of activity with a life of prayer. Their motto, *orare est laborare*—"to pray is to work"—expressed their ideal and was demonstrated in their practices. In such monasteries, the old culture of the classical Roman Empire, with its Latin and Greek literature, was preserved during a period when it might well have been altogether lost. One of the monasteries' great services was the copying of manuscripts, since printing had not yet been invented—and would not be until the fifteenth century when Gutenberg made the first printing press. So, all books had to be copied by hand. There still exist today thousands of beautifully handwritten manuscripts, often with lovely initialing, which show the great skill of some of the monks.

Besides preserving Western culture, monasteries provided hospitality for travelers, and cared for the sick in an age when there were no hospitals such as we know today. They intended to be godly examples of Christian life both in prayer and in action. And to a very considerable degree they succeeded in this aim, although naturally there were some houses and some monks and nuns that did not live up to the ideal—which explains why in the literature of the Middle Ages there are often satirical portrayals of them.

The Benedictines and most of the other religious orders practiced what was known as "the mixed life," which meant that they combined prayer and worship with manual labor or intellectual activity. But there were some, although few, orders which were purely contemplative. The members of such houses, including the Carthusians and others, devoted their entire time to worship or to private prayer. If God was the most important of all realities, then to "attend" to him (as they said) was the highest of all activities possible for man. So these orders withdrew from the world and its affairs, and made prayer—"the attentive presence of God"—absolutely central. From the houses where such monks and nuns lived came some of the most famous books on spiritual life, written out of deep personal experience.

Besides the established residential monastic houses, two orders of friars were also active. One of these had been founded by Saint Francis of Assisi; the Franciscans were itinerant preachers whose chief concern was to spread the gospel of Christ by word and to live a poor and humble life among the simple people, caring for the sick and looking after any in need. The other order was called the Order of Preachers, the followers of Saint Dominic, called Dominicans. This name was a pun, since it meant those who were Saint Dominic's disciples and also *domini canes*, "watchdogs of the Lord," so called because their founder had intended to defend the Catholic Christian faith against heretical groups such as the Albigensians, an ascetic and strange sect which for many years flourished especially in southern France. The Dominicans were concerned with learning. They were theologians who knew the faith and could both proclaim and defend it. This is the order which Thomas joined, becoming its greatest member, after the founder. Dominic himself was of Spanish descent, a most devout and holy man, and a friend of Saint Francis. At one time it had seemed that the two associations of friars (the word means "brothers") might be united, and Saint Dominic wished this to happen. But Saint Francis wanted a simpler, less learned sort of interest for his followers, and the union never came about.

Although the orders of friars did establish places of residence where they could study and teach, it was the monastic schools that were especially famous. Thomas attended the Benedictine school at Monte Cassino, and later became involved with some of the great universities which had become so important throughout Europe and in Britain. These universities were also very famous. In Britain, Oxford was flourishing; Cambridge was to be founded soon. On the Continent there was the great medical center at Salerno, south of Naples, and other universities in Italy, at Bologna, Naples, and Padua, among others. In France, the most famous was perhaps at Paris, but there were also universities at Montpelier and Grenoble. In Germany, there was Leipzig and Heidelberg, Basel in Switzerland, Prague in Bohemia, Vienna in Austria, and Cracow in Poland. Belgium had Louvain, and Spain and Portugal had Salamanca and Coimbra. Although all these countries did not exist under such names at the time, the universities were there.

The old universities had grown from the so-called cathedral-schools, academies which had been attached to the great diocesan churches, or they had come into existence around some great teacher. Perhaps some of them were simply started through associations of young men who desired further study. Each was famous for one or another special subject, such as Salerno's medical school. Paris had four faculties—arts (which included philosophy), canon law, theology, and medicine. Bologna was noted for its school of law, as were Padua and Orleans in France. Oxford was a theological and philosophical center.

The universities were quite different from those of today. In the first place, they were essentially groupings of students and teachers, with little of our modern formal organization and administrative arrangements. Teaching was, for the most part, lectures given by distinguished specialists, who depended for their livelihood on attracting numbers of young men to attend their discourses. There were no dormitories provided for the students; they found lodgings in hostels, often run by their masters or teachers, sometimes by others. Most of the students were poor boys, much younger than university people today. They lived simply— sometimes several of them had to share a room, sleeping on straw pallets—and they ate meager meals. They studied hard, but they also lived hard, too. There was a good deal of heavy drinking—wine, for the most part, since distilled spirits had not yet been invented—and quarrels between student groups were not infrequent. There were also fights between students and towns-people from time to time. Yet, on the whole, the medi-eval student was an earnest, honest, ambitious young man, anxious to master his subject and make a name for himself in the world of learning. We know a good deal about thirteenth-century students, since many of their letters, written to their homes and asking for clothing, money, or food supplies, have survived. These letters portray a hard life but a rewarding one for those who really wished to acquire knowledge.

The university curriculum was far different from twentieth-century schools. For the young man seeking his first degree, there was the so-called *trivium,* which included the ancient disciplines of grammar, rhetoric, and dialectic. Then there was advanced study, called the *quadrivium,* which would qualify the student to be a teacher. Examinations were conducted by the old scholastic method, in which the student would engage in discussion with others, using the dialectic of thesis and antithesis—or point and contrary point—which must then be resolved. The form in which Saint Thomas wrote his great *Summa Theologica* helps us to understand this: first, there is the statement of a problem, followed by the things which may be said for and against a possible solution, then the responses to those objections, and, finally, the resolution or sum-ming-up.

Another teaching device was used by Thomas in

some of his works. This was comment on the so-called *Sentences* (in Latin, this word means "opinions"). There were collections of these, such as Abelard's famous *Sic et Non,* or the *Sentences* of Peter Lombard. Series of important issues, opinions drawn from famous classical writers, philosophers, or theologians, were set down, often directly contradicting one another. The point was to talk about these—"comment on them," as it was then called—in an effort to reconcile them in some fashion or to show where errors might be found. This was a valuable exercise in sharpening wits and developing skill in argument.

Science as we now know it did not exist. What science there was simply described the facts of nature as they could be observed. Experiments in the modern sense were practiced only by alchemists, who mixed compounds in the hope of finding "the golden stone," an imaginary substance which, it was thought, conveyed almost magical powers. But alchemy, like astrology (the reading of destinies in the stars) was not approved by the truly learned, and was frowned upon in some ecclesiastical circles as playing with fire—going beyond the proper limits set for human knowledge. But curiosity was, of course, as lively then as now, and already there were some glimmerings of later experimental science, as (for instance) in Thomas' own great teacher Albertus Magnus.

While the ordinary parish priest did not attend a university, anyone who wished to achieve a position as a theologian was obliged to do so. The young men who thronged to hear Abelard at the University of Paris, and in the next century crowded the hall where Aquinas gave his lectures, were very likely intending to make theological study their lifework. If not that, they were hoping to teach philosophy or theology in a university, once they had acquired their rank as *magister artium,* "master (or teacher) of the arts." Some would go to the university simply because they had inquiring minds and no other particular vocation in life. It is said that there were some men who were "perpetual students" (as there are today), traveling from university to university, all over the Continent, simply to have the opportunity to listen to the great scholars. Such men were usually very poor. They lived from hand to mouth, but they were in love with knowledge for its own sake and they never tired of listening to the famous masters in Paris or Bologna, Prague or Salamanca. Some of the teachers also moved about a good deal, Thomas among them. His travels were requested by his superiors in the Order of Preachers, of course, but others simply went from place to place, possessed by a sort of wanderlust, or desire to see new places and to lecture to new students.

Thomas, the man and the teacher, was mainly interested in philosophy and theology. As such, he had to deal with the accepted system of Church *dogma.* Dogmas are brief statements of what the Church affirms to be true about God, his creation of the world and man; how man sinned by disobeying God; the uniting of God with man by His coming into the world in Jesus Christ; redemption or salvation through Christ; the Church as "the ark of salvation" and its worship and sacraments as the ways by which God strengthened and cared for his human children; the meaning of death; the state of purgatory after death where souls would be cleansed of what remained of their sins; and the final judgment, with the ultimate destiny of heaven or hell. All this was systematized and stated in propositions. Practically everybody believed this system of dogma. If he did not accept it, or questioned even some of it, he was likely to be very quiet about his disbelief or doubt.

The task of the philosopher was to show how this system could best be approached and argued for. The aim of the theologian was to continue the process of development, working out in more detail the implications of belief or their application to particular human problems. Thomas, like everyone else, had to take a stand on one or another of the prevalent ways of handling such matters.

What were the different ways among which a student or a thinker had to choose? What were the schools of thought which he must study, in order to select one, or to develop an approach of his own?

Roughly, they fell into four groups. The traditionally accepted school had grown out of the teaching of the great African theologian Augustine of Hippo

(Hippo was a town in Northern Africa, where he was bishop). Augustine had lived eight centuries or more before Thomas' time, but his influence was still very great. He was the son of a pagan father and a Christian mother, and he had grown up unbelieving. As a young man he had been attracted by Neo-Platonism, a widespread and popular philosophy in the Graeco-Roman world. It held that this world is a replica *in time* of what is always true in eternity, but the world distorts and misrepresents eternity. Everything proceeds from God who is pure Spirit. But in the world spirit is mixed with matter, a lesser form of being, and so a man must rise, or try to rise, above matter to the realm of pure spirit. In man's mind there is a reflection of that Spirit who is God, and in the world there are traces of the Spirit, too. When Augustine became a Christian he brought his Neo-Platonism and his new-found Christian faith together. The result is called Augustinianism. This was the traditional point of view in the Middle Ages, especially during the early part of that period.

The second school of thought showed the influence of the "two-kinds-of-truth" philosophy, which had entered Europe largely through Spain. For many years parts of Spain had been controlled by the Moors from northern Africa. They were Muslims, followers of the teaching of the Prophet Muhammad. Two very great Islamic, or Muslim, thinkers were Averroes and Avicenna. Their books were widely read and greatly respected. From them came a philosophy which claimed that human reason could not come to any such conclusions as Augustine had reached. Reason did not confirm Christian faith. Yet another kind of truth was given by God's revelation in the Church dogma. This was to be accepted on the authority of the Church, which was the authority of God. Human reason could attain only disbelief, but by faith one could still hold Christian beliefs. Not very many people took this view, but there were enough of them for Thomas to feel obliged to argue strongly against them. He did not believe that faith and this sort of skepticism could go together.

Thirdly, there were vast numbers of people—perhaps the majority—who simply refused to engage in this kind of speculative reasoning. Their main representative was Saint Bernard of Clairvaux, a holy and learned man with a very simple faith. For Bernard, and the many who agreed with him, it was entirely wrong to apply reason to matters of faith. Man should accept what the Church taught because God had disclosed it to the Church. This worked in practice, Bernard argued, producing good and holy lives, and it was not necessary to spend time in appealing to human reason.

Finally, there was the newly recovered Aristotelianism, which was beginning to influence the young men of the time.

Another kind of thought also gave Thomas much material for consideration. This was the controversy which raged in the universities between nominalism, realism, and conceptualism. Briefly, it was a question of whether any descriptive word is, or is not, a reflection of an eternal reality. For example, take the word *man*. Do we use this word simply as a convenient way of describing all men by the term "man" because they have certain similar characteristics? Or, when we say *man,* do we indicate that every man shares in something eternally true, a reality which is reflected in everyone we call by that word?

A *nominalist* (*nomen* is Latin for "name") agreed with the first position. A word is a convenient term to name thousands or millions of similar particular objects. A *realist* believed the second position, saying that we use the name "man" because we can identify every human being as reflecting *real* manhood, which is eternal and unchanging. Each particular man "participates" in manhood.

The third position between these two is called *conceptualism*. This view held that while there is, indeed, an eternal reality of "manhood," it can only be known because we know this man, that man, and the other man. Thomas agreed with this view and argued vigorously for it.

Or, put another way, the nominalist says that we observe the existence of a particular thing—in this case, men—and then we give it a class name—"man." A realist says that men all share in the reality of manhood. The word "man" only represents that true and unchanging reality, which was there before we gave it a name. A conceptualist says that while it is correct that there is a true reality of manhood, we know that only because we can see an individual man.

All of this may seem a somewhat silly controversy to us. However, in different form it still remains a very lively dispute among modern philosophers. The position adopted can make all the difference between complete skepticism about what we think men can know and some solid confidence that what we know is really true.

4.

Years of Study

AFTER Thomas arrived in Paris in 1245, he worked
with Albertus Magnus in the *studium generale* in the
French university. He attended the master's lectures
and produced what was called a *reportatio* of what he
heard. This was a reproduction, with annotations, of
what the teacher had said, and it served as a basis for
discussion. While much of the learning process in
the university consisted simply of attending lectures,
with careful attention to the teacher's words, another
important aspect of study was the discussion. The
teacher was present while his students engaged in a
methodical examination of each other's ideas.

A disputation, as such a discussion was called, was

not at all like a modern "bull session," in which any-body can speak and say what he thinks. Instead, there was a carefully followed order. Presiding over the session was a senior teacher. A given statement was announced, to which all discussion had to be directed. It might be something like this: "That by the use of man's reason, God's existence can be demonstrated." Those present then spoke on the subject. Very often objections were raised to the statement which was announced. Then an attempt would be made by others to provide answers to those objections. After a consider-able time spent in the presentation of the various ideas of the students, the presiding master would exercise his special privilege. This was to sum up the discussion, to restate the initial thesis or position, taking into account all the objections. Then he would attempt to deal with such criticisms in a way that would make the thesis clearer—or, if he happened to disagree with it, he would demolish it altogether.

If the presiding master had some junior assistants present, they would discuss and answer objections made by students. But in so doing, they would simply reply to comments without making any claim to con-clusive judgment on the points under discussion.

There is a story about Thomas in connection with one of these disputations, presumably at Cologne but perhaps in Paris. It concerns his first public defense of a thesis. The young friar set forth, as was customary, the various arguments for and against. Then he went on, in his enthusiasm, to propose certain distinctions in the meaning of words. These distinctions were to provide a definite solution to the problem. He dealt with the objections in a rather final fashion, violating the normal procedure in a disputation. At this point, Albertus, who was presiding, said, "Thomas, it appears that you yourself are not only discussing the question, which is your task, but are also deciding [determining, in the sense we have just indicated] the question as well." Having said this, he began to raise his own objections to what Thomas had been urging. To every objection, the young man had an answer—the chronicler says "a sufficient answer." At length Albertus exclaimed, "We call this lad a dumb ox, but I tell you that the whole world is going to hear his bellowing." After that disputation, Thomas was always chosen by Albertus to be responsible for the chief part in the more difficult disputations.

Thomas spent much time reading Aristotle and hearing lectures about him. The young friar also made a careful study of the classical work entitled *The Divine Names,* upon which Albertus was giving a series of lectures. This work was written several hundred years before by a thinker in the Hellenistic (Greek) world who had been converted to Christianity. He was known as Saint Denis. We now know that he adopted this name, as was the custom of the time, to secure an audience for his thought. Modern scholars call him "the Pseudo-Dionysius." His book is a study of the way in which human beings may think about and "give names" to God; that is, how human language may be applied to the divine being.

The Divine Names represents the Neo-Platonic way of thinking about Christianity, and is opposite from the Aristotelian way of dealing with such issues. Yet Thomas was able to assimilate the views of the Pseudo-Dionysius in such a way that he could find value in them and a use for them. This is shown in one of the few surviving documents written in Thomas' own hand—his summary of some of Albertus' lectures on *The Divine Names*.

Another book which Thomas studied is the great *Ethica* of Aristotle. Once again he worked through it under the guidance of Albertus, who was giving a course of lectures on Aristotle's ethical ideas. Some twenty years later, Thomas wrote his own commentary on the same book, in which he shows astonishing mastery of the text and an ability to question it at point after point, even while he accepts the main thesis—that every man, in determining what is good, seeks happiness as his end, although the kind of happiness he seeks will establish the sort of man that he is becoming. Thomas takes this thesis and uses it in a specifically Christian way. Presumably, he had long been pondering the ideas, since he had read the book as a student. Actually, all of his writing gives evidence of long thought, careful consideration, and precision in putting down his conclusions. There is nothing hasty or shoddy, nor does Thomas ever attempt to gain an easy victory by seizing on the weak points of a view that he is criticizing. He was a fair opponent, and he always allowed his intellectual foe to have his say, while at the same time he was very sharp in criticism and able to detect a flaw in his opponent's argument. Even those who disagree with his conclusions must admit that, as a thinker, he was honest, fair, and glad to give other positions a genuine hearing.

Since Thomas was so silent in the university, one of his fellow students thought that he must be singularly stupid. Therefore, the student offered, after one of the lectures, to explain what Albertus Magnus (who was talking about *The Divine Names*) had been expounding. With courtesy, Thomas accepted the offer and listened to the exposition. At some point along the way, however, his companion faltered in his explanation. Thomas took it up and continued the account with great clarity and with some of his own critical comments. The other young man was astounded. So this silent young Italian was not so unintelligent as he had thought. He reported the incident to the student master, the member of the Dominican hostel in charge of students, saying, "That Neapolitan Thomas knows a great deal. He explained Master Albert's lecture to me today; and I confess that he did it so well that I understand it better than when I tried to see what the Master himself was saying." Thomas' silence, to say the least, was deceptive.

Thomas spent six or seven years with Albertus, at Paris and later at Cologne. In 1252, his studies were completed as far as ordinary university courses were concerned. He returned to Paris to receive his degree of bachelor of theology. He would, of course, continue his academic career, working toward the degree of magister, official recognition of his teaching authority.

Despite the very impersonal way in which Thomas, in his later writings, gives expression to his ideas, there can be no doubt of his close relationship to Albertus. He does not indicate this indebtedness in so many words, but the influence of the older man was obviously very great. We have no record of Thomas' personal feelings for Albertus, but there are a number of references which show the master's devotion to the young man who studied with him.

The two men were very different in character and in natural genius. Yet they were united in the aim of bringing the wisdom of the world's thinkers into relationship with Christian faith. This close association is beautifully illustrated in Dante's poem *The Divine Comedy,* where the poet has Thomas introduce Albertus, as they stand side by side in heaven, calling Albertus "brother and master" (*Paradiso,* x, 98).

After Thomas' return to Paris, in 1252, to begin his work as a bachelor, the two men were separated, save for very infrequent meetings, particularly at the general chapters of the Dominican Order. It is likely that they spent a short time together at Valenciennes, where plans were made by the order for a revision of its entire program of study. They may also have seen a little of each other during the years when Thomas was at Orvieto, not far from Rome, from 1261 to 1263. At that time, Albertus was attached to the papal court.

Before Thomas went to Paris in 1252, he had been ordained to the priesthood, although the actual date is not known. There is also evidence that he was offered the abbacy of the religious house of Monte Cassino. The offer of this post, which Thomas refused, was made "as a favor to Thomas' parents," so it is said. Since his father had died in 1244, the reference must be to the Lady Theodora. The fortunes of the Aquino family had been reduced, largely because some of its members had been implicated in a rebellion against the Holy Roman Emperor. Perhaps the offer was made to assist in the restoration of the family's reputation. In any event, Thomas refused the offer. To become abbot of the Benedictine monastery would have meant leaving the Dominican Order to join the Benedictines, and this he would never do. It was possible although not common to transfer from one religious community to another, but such a change would not have appealed to Thomas Aquinas.

There was some hesitation in the high circles of the Dominicans about appointing Thomas to the post of bachelor lecturing in Paris. Albertus proposed his name, but the master general at that time did not yet realize the remarkable ability of the young man whom he had befriended during the troubles at Monte San Giovanni and Roccasecca. When the master general seemed hesitant, Albertus called in as another reference a noted teaching friar, Hugh of Saint Cher, who himself had held a master's chair at the University of Paris. The master general was influenced by this recommendation, since Hugh was a greatly respected teacher, the second Dominican to occupy the responsible theological chair in Paris. In later years he became the first member of his order to be elevated to the rank of cardinal at the papal court.

When Thomas began lecturing in Paris, he was only twenty-six, but he made an excellent impression. During his first year, he lectured mostly on the Bible. Then he gave his two-year course on the *Sentences* of Peter Lombard. At this time he also began to write books. The first of these, doubtless based on the lectures he gave, was a series of commentaries on four books on the *Sentences*. He also wrote two smaller works—"Concerning the principles of nature" and "Concerning being and essence." The titles indicate the direction of his thinking. He was interested in philosophical problems as they might be explored in understanding the world and its nature. Both titles also have an Aristotelian ring; and this is, in fact, the sort of approach which Thomas took. These three books began to bring to Thomas the fame that gave him his prominent position in the intellectual world of the time.

The young teacher was not only occupied with his lectures and his writings, however. He found himself caught up in a controversy then raging in Paris. There was considerable hostility in the city to both the Dominican and Franciscan orders, largely from the so-called secular (nonmonastic) clerical teachers and masters in the university faculty of theology. The two religious orders were insistent on their right to be represented on the university staff; the Dominicans especially, since their whole purpose as an order was to present and defend the Christian faith. Unless they had a real and secure position in Paris, their aims could not be realized. How could they hope to defend the faith if they did not enjoy full membership in the great university center of theology? The controversy was eventually resolved in favor of the two orders, but it must have been difficult to work in a situation where hostility was so apparent.

In 1256, Thomas was given his licentiate in theology. This meant that he was now a recognized expert in the subject, having proved his competence by four years of teaching. The following year he was admitted to the corporation of magistri, or official masters of instruction, in the University of Paris. (This took place during a lull in the controversy between the orders and the secular members of the faculty.) A letter still exists, addressed to the chancellor of the university, in which Pope Alexander IV offered his congratulations on Thomas' appointment. In the letter the pope speaks of Thomas as "a man of noble birth and evident integrity of character, who by God's grace has amassed a treasure of learning and knowledge." Since Thomas became a master when he was about thirty-one years old—the customary age was thirty-five —his admission is in itself an indication of the competence he had shown and of the high respect which was felt for him.

Thomas impressed his students as a man whose "mind was full of new light from God." This is the phrase which Gui uses in his biography. He also says that Thomas' teaching "seemed novel to them, with new arrangements of the subject matter, new methods of proof, and new arguments adduced for the conclusions." Thomas was impatient with the older and more stilted way of teaching. He wished to interest the students and involve them more deeply in their subjects. Instead of following the old set patterns, he developed new ones, working always from the two sources which his study of Aristotle had given him—the appeal to ordinary human experience, and the rigorous use of reason, following a logical development and insisting on careful attention to whether or not a conclusion followed properly from a previous assertion. This meant that Thomas was not content simply to appeal to some ancient authority as a final answer to whatever question was up for discussion. He wanted to know whether or not that answer was in agreement with experience, and whether or not it could be defended by sound argument.

There is no doubt that this approach, while it stimulated and excited the young students, annoyed and dismayed some of the older members of the faculty. It questioned their established method of teaching, and it opened up the possibility of doubting ideas which they had long taken for granted. It is no wonder, therefore, that some of the older men were opposed to this independent young lecturer, who ventured to alter methods of teaching and to introduce new ideas.

When the time came for Thomas to give his inaugural lecture—his first public appearance as a recognized magister of the university—he was very nervous and uncertain of what he should say. Not only was he well below the usual age, but he was also conscious of the opposition felt by some of the older masters. He had tried to excuse himself from appointment at that time, pleading that he was too young and that he was not sufficiently learned. But his appeal had been overruled and the appointment made, some sources say on orders from the papal representatives. Now he was to face the entire faculty, who gathered to hear each inaugural lecture. What should be his subject? How should he approach it?

One night, not too long before the appointed day, Thomas had a dream in which an old Dominican asked him why he was so troubled in spirit. Thomas answered that his agitation was due to the lecture which he must give and his uncertainty about both topic and method of approach. The old man told him not to be afraid; he also suggested a topic for the lecture. When Thomas awoke, he felt refreshed in mind and spirit. He lectured on the suggested topic and managed to get through his ordeal with little or no trouble. This incident was used later on as evidence of a special visitation by God to the new magister. Whatever we may think about that interpretation, certainly Thomas' experience was the kind that may well take place when someone is much troubled about a problem, and, in a dream state, a solution seems offered. The text suggested to Thomas in his dream is from Psalm 104, verse 14 (in the usual English version—Psalm 103, quoted in the Latin Vulgate text of the Bible which Thomas would have used) : "He watereth the hills from above; the earth is filled with the fruit of thy works."

During the three years which followed his incorporation into the University of Paris as a magister, Thomas continued his lecturing—now on a greater variety of topics—and also went on with his writing. A good deal of the famous *Summa contra Gentiles,* the defense of Christianity against philosophical attack, was written during this period. So also were his commentary on the Old Testament Book of Isaiah—doubtless based once more on lectures given on the Holy Scriptures— and two of his best-known shorter books. These are a commentary on a famous theological work by the earlier writer Boethius dealing with God as Holy Trinity, and a discussion of the nature of truth called the *De Veritate*. The second book is one of Thomas' most brilliant and incisive works, concerned with the nature of truth, the way in which truth is to be stated, and how it may be arrived at by the mind of man. Some have said that in it one finds, in miniature, most of the author's distinctive thought.

In 1259, Thomas went to the general chapter of the Dominicans, held at Valenciennes for the purpose of revising the program of studies for members of the order. He then went on to Italy, where he spent the next year as a preacher general for the Roman Province, or division, of the Order of Preachers. Both of the earliest sources about his life say that he preached only in Italian. Therefore, most of his sermons must have been preached on this and other visits to Italy. Some of them are preserved. They seem to have been prepared with fairly simple congregations in mind, since they are quite short, filled with scriptural references, and always very much to the point. In this they reflect what Thomas himself once wrote on the matter of sermons: "If short they are much more likely to be acceptable, because if they are good they are heard the more eagerly and if they are bad the boredom does not last very long." That comment is another indication of Thomas' gentle wit, as well as proof of his ability to understand the attitude of the ordinary person, who is by no means an intellectual and grasps ideas more

73

easily when they are put in simple and short sentences.

Thomas wrote, taught, and spoke in Latin when he was engaging in his academic work as a Dominican. But except for his native Italian, he does not seem to have been able to speak any other languages. One of his biographers explains this by saying that Thomas was so busy and so much engaged in "continual abstraction" (presumably, this means in deep thought) that he had no free time to learn other languages.

Thomas' homilies, or talks, addressed to members of his religious order at their services of worship, were also in Latin. These talks were given in the evening, just before the community supper. They were known as *collationes,* a word which is also used to describe the light evening-meal itself. Some of the homilies make very good reading even today. Like his sermons, they are short and to the point. Thomas would also read the famous collection of *Homilies of the Fathers,* popular in religious houses of the day. He was able to expound such material, as well as biblical passages (especially from the gospels and from Saint Paul's letters), with great ease and remarkable clarity.

After his year as a preacher general, Thomas went to Orvieto, to serve as a member of the papal court under Pope Urban IV. Orvieto is one of the most charming of Italian hill towns, just off the main road between Rome and Siena. It stands on a high hill, surrounded by walls that survive even today from medieval times. The only way to reach the town is by a road

74

that winds steeply around the hill. From the town walls there is a sharp drop of perhaps five hundred feet to the plain below. Orvieto then had its magnificent new cathedral, whose facade still delights visitors. The papal palace is behind the cathedral, at the right side, with a garden that goes to the walls and provides a magnificent view of the surrounding countryside. Thomas lived there from 1261 to 1264.

In residence at Orvieto, he was able to continue his writing without interruption. He completed the *Summa contra Gentiles,* wrote biblical commentaries (on the Epistles of Saint Paul to the Romans and Corinthians), and also a critique of certain aspects of Greek thought, called *Contra errores Graecorum* ("Against the errors of the Greeks"). He had been succeeded in Paris by the young man who had served as bachelor under him, the Roman Romano de Rossi Orsini, a nephew of Pope Nicholas III. Evidently Romano did not agree with Thomas in certain respects. He was more of an Augustinian (or follower of a Platonic type of thought) than Thomas had been, although he had spent some time in Paris as Thomas' assistant.

While Thomas was in Orvieto, he was asked by the pope to prepare the special services for the new feast of Corpus Christi. The reason for establishing a new day in the Church's holy-day calendar was a miracle said to have taken place not too far from Orvieto. There a priest who doubted the true presence of Christ in the

Holy Communion was given, by certain signs, unde-
niable proof of the fact. The service Thomas prepared
contains some of his best-known Latin hymns, a selection from verses of Scripture, and some prayers. It is
used even today on Corpus Christi day in the Roman
Catholic Church. Parts of it are also used for the service
held in connection with the "adoration" and "benediction" of the sacrament, during which the consecrated
bread is exposed, those present engage in worship of
Christ present, and appropriate prayers and hymns are
sung.

A year after this work was completed, in 1265,
Thomas went to the city of Rome, under appointment
as regent, or director, of the provincial school of studies
of the Dominicans. The school was at the Church of
Santa Sabina, which still stands. For two years he continued this work, having responsibility for the arrangement of courses of instruction, supervision of the whole
program of training the younger members of the order,
and also giving lectures on some of the required subjects. But he was still able to continue his own writing.
He began the preparation of a series of commentaries
on the books of Aristotle, a project which was naturally
very dear to his heart. He wrote three of his smaller
works on questions which were then under discussion
in theological circles. Above all, he found time in the
midst of his busy life to begin writing his great second
Summa. This was the *Summa Theologica*—"the theological summary," in which he planned to discuss the

entire theological teaching of the Church. Work on the *Summa* continued until a few months before his death on 1274. He was never able to complete it, although a disciple finished the last section so that it appeared as a full presentation of Catholic theology.

Throughout his life, Thomas often traveled in Europe. He must have had prodigious energy, because such trips were by no means easy. Of course, they were all undertaken by direction of his superiors. As an obedient member of his order, Thomas would not hesitate to go where he was sent. Yet, the journeys must have been tiring. Friars in the thirteenth century tramped all over Europe on roads which were poor at best and indescribably bad at worst. Thomas went from Naples to Paris, from Paris to Cologne and back again; from Paris to Italy; frequent trips from city to city in Italy; a terrible march from Viterbo in Italy and back to Paris. He might have visited Britain, but this is uncertain. All of his travels (except for the one brief sea voyage) were on foot; he carried his possessions (such as they were) with him. Thomas bore up under bad weather, even when it meant striding through heavy rain until he could find some shelter. His trips were in the company of other friars, since it was not customary for members of the religious orders to travel alone. Nonetheless, they were unpleasant—day after day and week after week of walking, stopping only at night in some religious house or, if there were no house available, at a peasant's cottage, eating only the food that was offered—for the friars were "poor men," not permitted to amass money which might buy them substantial meals—and never certain of a good night's rest because of the long distances between towns. All of this is some indication of the physical endurance of a man whose whole nature was more academic and intellectual than that of many of his fellow friars.

In the year 1267, the new pope, Clement IV, called Thomas to join him at Viterbo, not very far from Rome. Thomas spent almost two years there, during which time he was offered the archbishopric of Naples. Although he loved the city, he refused the offer. Thomas believed that his vocation was in writing and teaching, not in ecclesiastical administration. But the offer was a great honor to him and to his order. Again there is some evidence that one of the reasons for the suggestion was to assist Thomas' family, who were still suffering financially.

During these years Thomas was called to preach from time to time in the churches of Rome. There are records of his having preached in the great Saint Peter's, as well as in the basilica of Santa Maria Maggiore, which still stands in the city as one of the largest and most beautiful of the ancient basilicas. The Saint Peter's where Thomas preached has been replaced by the present magnificent basilica.

At Viterbo Thomas continued his work on the *Summa Theologica* and completed some further discussions of "disputed questions." He also found time to carry on with his projected commentary on the works of Aristotle. But much of his time was spent in theological business at the papal court.

In 1268, Thomas was recalled to Paris, where he resumed his lecturing. These next three years were among the most productive in his life. Not only did he write the second major section of the *Summa Theologica,* but he also produced two books on philosophical subjects—one on "the eternity of the world" and another on "the unity of the intellect." He was able to do commentaries on three of Aristotle's most important works, especially Aristotle's *Metaphysics,* as well as finish his commentary on Aristotle's *Ethics.*

It seems amazing that in such a relatively short time, Thomas could have written so many books, especially learned books which contained such careful argument and precise reasoning. According to one of his early biographers, he accomplished this by giving "a minimum of time to sleeping and eating, and all the rest to prayer or reading or thinking or writing or dictating." There is much evidence that a good deal of Thomas' writings was dictated to a secretary, who wrote down what the master said, prepared a fair copy, and then submitted it for correction before it was made available to the reading public. But even that would require time and effort, and perhaps the biographer is correct when he says that Thomas could accomplish so much because he had both "natural intelligence and the habit of study," coupled with a remarkable capacity to concentrate on the subject.

Through all those busy years Thomas also took part in the ordered and regular life of the religious houses in which he was resident. This included the saying of a daily mass—which he did "very devoutly," that is, slowly and carefully—as well as assisting other members of the order when it was their time to celebrate the mass. There were the Breviary services as well, which all members of the order were required to say daily. There were appointed periods for private prayer and for meditation, and hours given to conversation, in which all the residents were expected to join. Thomas must have lived a very well-regulated and orderly life, for in addition to his religious duties, writing, and teaching, he found time to give his students an occasional outing and to provide a banquet for them at the end of their academic course.

Thomas Aquinas lived only about fifty years, yet those years were filled with activity. And he seemed never to be hurried or harassed. Thomas had truly learned how to use his time and energies to his best advantage.

5.

The Last Years

THOMAS was very happy during his teaching years in Paris. He had lived there from time to time, he knew the city and the university, and he would, doubtless, have been pleased to remain there for many years. But once again, duty called him to another post.

In 1272, the chapter, or annual meeting, of the Dominicans in Italy was held at Florence. Three years before, it had been decided to open two new schools of study, one at Orvieto and the other at Naples. The chapter decided that Thomas was the man to organize the Naples school. He did not wish to leave his work in Paris, and it is clear that the younger members of the university did not want him to go away, but, of course, he went to Naples as ordered.

Thomas traveled on foot from Florence to Naples immediately after the chapter was adjourned. He was already familiar with the hostel for Dominicans, since he had studied there in his youth at the university. At once he took up his duties, arranging the courses of study, securing the staff to give them, and spending much time in administrative work that was not particularly attractive to him.

But Thomas still had time to continue his writing. Despite his new responsibilities, he also concentrated on his own studies. He wrote two more commentaries on the books of Aristotle and he also gave attention to the completion of the *Summa Theologica*.

A great deal of existing material about Thomas concerns his last period in Naples. Much of it is legendary, but nevertheless it gives us a good insight into the sort of impression that Thomas made on those who were with him, knew him well, and loved him dearly.

For one thing, his absentmindedness comes out clearly. One story tells of a visit to Naples by "a certain cardinal legate, recently arrived from Sicily," who wished to have an interview with the regent. Thomas sat down between the cardinal and the archbishop of Naples, who had arranged the meeting. But his mind was miles away and, as usual, he did not speak. The other two men also kept silent. The cardinal wondered why Thomas paid so little attention to him and his fellow dignitary, but the archbishop whispered that

82

Thomas was often like that when his mind was absorbed in a problem. Then Thomas' face lighted up, and he exclaimed, "Ah, now I've got it!" The archbishop took hold of Thomas' cloak and tugged it, saying, "Wake up, Master. Here's the cardinal legate who has come here on purpose to see you." At once Thomas came out of his fit of abstraction, bowed reverently to the cardinal and asked his pardon. He explained that he had thought he was still in his cell, working on an important question. The problem was so enthralling that he had been unaware of leaving the cell to see visitors.

Another story concerns the cauterization (the burning away of injured tissue) of one of his legs. The doctors did the job as quickly as possible, in order not to pain the friar too much. But they need not have bothered. Thomas was so deep in thought that he was almost entirely unconscious of what was going on.

While in Naples, Thomas did a considerable amount of popular preaching in Italian. His words "had a warmth in them that kindled the love of God and sorrow for sin in men's hearts." He is also said to have been very gentle with others, finding it hard to believe in the sins of his fellowmen. When he reached the point where he had to admit wrongdoing, it was as if he himself had done the wrong, and he grieved as if the sin were his own.

Late in 1273, Thomas received a summons from Pope Gregory X. This time he was to go to Lyons in southern France, to be present at a great conference. Representatives of both the Greek, or Eastern, Orthodox and the Roman Catholic Church were to discuss ways in which the two groups, who had been divided, might once again be reunited. Thomas was directed to bring with him the treatise which he had prepared years before at Orvieto, on "the errors of the Greeks." It was probably thought that his research and his answers to what the western (or Catholic) Christians regarded as mistakes in the theology of the eastern (or Greek Orthodox) Christians could serve as a basic for discussion.

Thomas was not in good health. He had worked altogether too hard for too many years. He was tired and his physical strength was depleted. Furthermore, a recent and profound religious experience, the nature of which we do not know, had so much preoccupied him that he did not feel any great interest in the theological questions which were to be debated. Yet, as a loyal son of the Church, he undertook this new responsibility. So, he set out in late January or possibly early February of 1274. Reginald, his faithful friend and fellow Dominican, and a lay brother, James of Salerno, went with him.

The three followed the main road, stopping for rest from time to time. Just beyond the town of Capua, at the point where the road makes a descent from Teano to Borgonuova, the ailing friar struck his head against a tree that had fallen across the way. Yet, he was able to continue the journey, passing Monte Cassino and his childhood home at Roccasecca, and then turning toward the coast to take the Via Appia northward.

The friars stopped at Maenza to visit Francesca, Thomas' niece. But now Thomas was unable to continue; he was seriously ill. When it became clear that his condition was very grave, he asked to be carried to the monastery of Fossa Nova, so that he might die in a religious house.

The abbey of Fossa Nova is on the slopes of the Monti Lepini, overlooking a valley, and it has a very long history. It was actually founded by monks from Savoy in France, although legend says that it goes back to the first days of Benedictine monasticism. The stone of the abbey is mellowed with age, and the church was consecrated by Pope Innocent III in 1208.

As Thomas was brought into the religious house in March, 1274, he quoted a favorite psalm: "Here will be my rest forever; here will I dwell because I delight in it." He probably had come to love the place from his former visits. Certainly he was on intimate terms with the Cistercian monks who lived there.

Thomas was at once taken to the cell reserved for those who were ill. He remained quietly on his pallet, never complaining although he was evidently in a much weakened condition. He became more and more obviously ill, and it was apparent that little could be done for him. He did not speak much, even to Reginald, who remained with him.

However, Thomas did make one request. He asked that one book of the Old Testament be read to him from beginning to end. The book is the so-called Song of Solomon. Originally it was a long love-poem, written by an ancient Hebrew to the woman he loved. It had been included, along with much else, in the Old Testament, and thus formed part of the sacred literature of the Jewish people. When the Old Testament was taken over by the Christian Church, this love lyric was taken also. But now it was regarded as a beautiful allegory of the relationship between Christ and his Church. It was also used as a kind of statement of the relationship between a Christian believer and his Lord.

With that interpretation, the Song of Solomon was used in the Middle Ages as a guide to men of faith in deepening their love of Jesus Christ. No doubt, that is why Thomas wished to have it read to him, for he took it as a lovely allegory of what one might call the love affair between a Christian and God who is disclosed in Christ.

The reading was done slowly so that Thomas could follow the words. A little later, he asked for one of the priests to hear his confession. Since he apparently knew that death was upon him, he wished to receive the last sacrament. The priest came, everyone else left the room, and Thomas made his confession. Then he was given the Holy Communion, which, as he believed, became through God's act, the very life of Jesus Christ himself.

The hours drew on. Reginald returned to the room and remained with Thomas and the priest who had heard his confession and administered the sacrament. Finally, on March 7, 1274, as quietly and as simply as he had lived, Thomas of Aquino died.

The room in which Thomas died was later enlarged into a chapel, to be a place of pilgrimage. It contains an altar with a Latin inscription. The whole shrine was conceived in the seventeenth century by Cardinal Ippolito Aldobrandini, who was a "commendatory abbot" of the house at Fossa Nova.

Because Thomas had taught in Paris and had been so important to the Dominican house of studies attached to the university, the university authorities wanted his body to be buried in that city. But it was decided to bury him instead at the Church of Saint Sernin in Toulouse, in southern France. The Dominican Order had been very active in that part of France. The tomb of Saint Thomas at Toulouse became a place of pilgrimage, just as many of the cities where he had lived or preached soon had their own special places to honor him.

Thomas Aquinas was dead, having lived less than fifty years. Stories soon grew up about "miracles" he was said to have performed after his death. And some years later, this hardworking, devoted, modest and unassuming, yet strangely attractive, man would be called a saint.

6.

The Synthesis Between Christian Faith and Philosophy

To understand the synthesis which Saint Thomas Aquinas made between Christian faith and the new philosophy of his time, as well as his attempt to work out a system that would cover all of the knowledge and experience of men, it is important to understand the two characteristics of this man.

First, Thomas was a very devout and a very convinced Christian. He had been born into a family which not only accepted the Christian faith but practiced it. The society in which he lived was founded upon that faith. He was trained in a Benedictine monastery and later in the Order of Preachers. His daily life had only deepened his faith, and he was himself a pious person. He engaged in personal prayer and the other elements in Christian life which are intended to develop genuine devotion.

Second, Saint Thomas was a man of extraordinary common sense. He actually used those words on occasion to appeal to the ordinary ideas by which ordinary people live their ordinary day-by-day lives. And he was very hardheaded about this. He had no use for flights into fancy, and he would never let his better judgment be overruled by sentimental notions or by what one might like to be true.

As a result of his devout Christian faith and his commonsense approach, Saint Thomas had little use either for a too simple acceptance of the Church dogmas or for an escape from the reality of the world. He did not believe that Christian traditions should be accepted without looking at them and thinking about them. He did accept the faith, but he did not accept it in a simplistic way. He thought that a man should try to understand what that faith was, how it had come to be, and why it should be believed. This is why Thomas got into trouble at various times in his life, and why, for a short time after his death, his views were regarded as dangerous. But Saint Thomas Aquinas was a rationalist, who thought that men had been given reason to be used and not to be rejected when it came to religious matters.

Saint Thomas also opposed the idea that being a

Christian meant to run away from the realities of this world. Therefore, he could not agree with the traditional thought of his time, which regarded the world as so distorted by sin and so marked by inadequacy and evil that it was best for people not to think about it, and, instead, concentrate on the realm of pure spirit. Saint Thomas thought that since man is in the world, since he has human reason, he must look at the world as it is, wrestle with the problems it presents to him, and hold his Christian faith because that faith does not destroy or reject the world of nature. In his own words, "Grace [the realm of spiritual things] does not destroy nature; on the contrary, it perfects it."

Thomas was not skeptical about man's knowledge of the world. He was convinced that we can know a great deal about the world around us, and that we can bring the Christian faith into a meaningful relationship with that world. Here again, he was a rationalist, a man with very great confidence in the capacity of human reason to discover truth. And reason would discover truth, not because it was somehow supernaturally guided, but because, in and of itself, the human mind is able to think soundly and to reach valid conclusions.

Of course, Thomas recognized that the human mind can make mistakes and that these mistakes are often very serious indeed. He asked only that man use his mind as honestly as possible. He should check and recheck all his thinking by seeing what other people have thought. Thinking was not a completely individualistic matter for Thomas. To think rightly demanded that we find out what other men thought, so that our personal ideas may be corrected or expanded in the light of *common* thought.

In this way, too, Thomas was realistic. Most people do live and think by checking their own ideas against what others have to tell them. They are not like the old man who said to his wife, "Everybody is wrong but you and me; and sometimes I think you are wrong, too." That kind of individualism is an impossible position in ordinary life.

For Thomas Aquinas, Christian faith that was devoutly believed, and common sense that was honestly accepted, produced a temper of mind that was both believing and courageous. And Thomas' approach to the world was both humble and bold. It is said that the nineteenth-century scientist Thomas Henry Huxley once wrote to a friend that "one must sit down before the fact and let it teach one its lesson." That was also Thomas' attitude. Look at the facts, he would say, and learn from them; then think as courageously as you can about what they have taught you.

"Facts" for Thomas included not only nature and human beings, but also the faith the Church taught— a faith that presumably is also based on facts. He was prepared to think courageously about these facts. His synthesis—his vision of the whole of reality from God to the dust of the earth—is the result of that courageous thinking. That synthesis may not be workable for modern men and women, but no thinking person would deny the courage, honesty, and extraordinary intellectual powers with which Thomas undertook the job. His synthesis is impressive in the broad sweep of his vision, and it is one of the grand constructions of the human mind, deserving great respect, if not universal acceptance.

Thomas was especially opposed to any philosophy or religion which said that this world is in itself evil. He recognized that there is much that is wrong in the world, and he was sure that men and women were prone to be sinners, as the Christian faith said. But the world itself was God's creation, and, therefore, it could not be evil simply because it was not as perfect as God himself. To say that, in Thomas' time, was to contradict a great many people. Throughout history, many people have held a negative attitude about the world, and especially in the early days of the Christian Church. Unfortunately, this outlook entered Christian thinking and continued to affect much of it. Within the Church, it resulted in a kind of world rejection, which today we call puritanism. Outside the Christian Church, in its first few hundred years, there developed a *Manichaean* streak against which great Christian thinkers waged continual warfare.

The Manichaeans were a pagan sect who believed that there were two powers in the universe. One was the good power, the good god; the other was the evil power, which had taken complete control of the world. The only way in which good people could live, therefore, was to say a loud no to the world. It was a bad place, it was evil, and it must be rejected if a man hoped to find God and live a good life. Saint Thomas Aquinas regarded that attitude as utterly un-Christian, and he was also sure that it was completely wrong on rational grounds.

According to one story, Thomas was dining in the royal banquet hall of King Louis of France. Louis was a devout Christian (he was later canonized and we know him as Saint Louis the Good of France) , and he was anxious to entertain the distinguished scholar. During dinner, Thomas was quiet as usual, and he seemed to be in deep thought throughout the meal. Then, to everyone's amazement, he suddenly brought down his fist on the table, making it shake and the goblets and dishes jump. As he did this, he said in a loud voice, *"That* will settle the Manichaeans!"

Throughout the meal, Thomas had undoubtedly been deep in thought about the negative attitude of the Manichaeans' position. Then he had seen a way of showing the falsity of that position. In his excitement at this discovery, he had cried out and banged the table. That incident is typical of Thomas' capacity to concentrate on a subject. It also shows how deeply he opposed the Manichaean view.

Thomas believed in the worth of the world. He was convinced that deep down it is a good world, both because God made it and because men find goodness in it. He believed that the only healthy attitude toward life is a positive one, finding value in the ordinary things that surround us. And since he believed this, at the same time believing that human reason could be trusted, he sought an argument to prove this value of the world. At that dinner table, he felt that he had found the argument. Although we do not have the details of the argument, the whole synthesis that Thomas created was basically a way in which the goodness of creation is demonstrated and the worth of this world and of human life is upheld.

In his system, Thomas portrays the world as two-leveled. One level is the natural order of things, the created world in which we live and which we try to understand in human terms. The other level is the supernatural order, which is not against the world level or in complete contradiction to it. Rather, it is above (supernatural, from the Latin words *supra* or *super*, means "above" or "over"). The supernatural world is God himself and God's activity.

How can we know these two levels? The natural world can be known through human experience and through human reason, which tries to make sense of that experience. The supernatural world can be known only by revelation, which means by God's disclosing himself and his plans to us. The human mind is able to understand what God reveals; otherwise, there would be no sense in talking about his revelation, for revelation always signifies somebody telling something to somebody. So, God discloses the truth about himself to us. If we could not achieve some understanding about what God tells us, it would be silly to talk of a revelation.

Saint Thomas also believed that by the use of human reason we can discover that God does exist. As he said, by reason we can discover that God is; by revelation we are told *what* God is. Human reason can arrive at the fact that there is a God who is the final and complete explanation of everything. But when it comes to knowing God's character, his creative purpose in the world, and what he desires men to be like and to do, we must depend upon God's revealing these things to us. There are hints or suggestions of God's creative power in our experience. There are also hints or suggestions of what he is "up to" in the world. But these are only hints and suggestions; they do not give us absolutely certain knowledge. For that, God himself must inform us. Thomas believed that God had done that through the history of the Jewish people, in Jesus Christ in whom God has "become man," and through the experience and teaching of the Church.

How do we know anything at all? This was a question that concerned Thomas very deeply, and he thought and wrote a great deal about it. His answer was that the human mind is created in such a fashion that it is capable of grasping things outside itself. And, in turn, things in the world have a capacity to be

known. Thomas called this capacity *intelligible species.*
Truth, for Saint Thomas, is the meeting of the capacity
to be known and our capacity to know. He called that
meeting *adaequatio*—the equation, or union, of the
actual facts in the world with our minds which seek to
know the facts.

Man does not always have accurate knowledge of
truth, but that is because he does not see the facts as
they really are. One way of correcting this is to compare what we think with what other people think. This
will help to remove individual errors. For example, you
look at a table and see it only from your own perspective. Yet, it is a real table that you see. Other people
see it from their perspectives, although they are looking at the same table. When people get together and
compare notes they have an accurate idea of what the
table really is, making allowances for the differences in
perspective.

This may seem very complicated, but all Thomas is
saying is that we should trust our experience, given us
through our senses, allowing for the mistakes which
are due to being in one place rather than in another.
We should respect what our arguments can lead us
to see, always allowing for mistakes in our logic or way
of arguing. In believing this, Thomas was following
the treatment of human mental processes, which he had
learned from his study of Aristotle.

Aristotle was a pupil of the great Plato, but he was
also a thinker in his own right. A practical man, he had

much interest in the world of nature. In fact, he was a kind of very early scientific observer. He also had great respect for common sense. He was prepared to trust his experience, and he was equally prepared to accept the capacity of the human mind to do sound and accurate thinking. His writings (for the most part notes that his students took down as he lectured) were very influential for hundreds of years. Then, they were somehow lost, so far as European thought was concerned. But in Asia Minor they were preserved, and when the Muslims conquered that part of the world they were so deeply impressed by Aristotle's writings that they studied them carefully. Thus, Aristotle became very important in Muslim thinking and many acute philosophers called him *the* philosopher. In Saint Thomas' time, Aristotle was known as "the master of those who know."

Through the spread of information and literature from Spain—which the Moors largely controlled—into the rest of Europe, Aristotle once again became a man whose writings were to be taken very seriously. Also, the Crusades, which had opened the door for influences from Asia Minor to Europe, helped to spread his fame.

Aristotle differed in many ways from Plato. He seemed to threaten the overturn of ideas which had been taken for granted among Christians for hundreds of years. Aristotle did not talk about the world and God in the familiar terms of a creation that dimly

97

reflected the pure Spirit who is God. Instead, he talked about the world as set in motion—started going, we might say—by an unmoved First Mover—God himself. He talked of God as the First Cause, who had given the impetus for all the other causes and effects which we see in the world. He talked of God as absolutely and completely unchanged and unchangeable, contrasting God with the world where everything is changeable and changing. For Aristotle, God was so "unmoved" that He never did anything personally. He moved the world and he provided the "first cause," just because he was, not because he acted. He was sheer thought, pure mind. Everything else was dependent upon him for its existence.

This may seem very abstract, and, of course, it is. That is why so many of Thomas' contemporaries were worried about Aristotle's writings. How, they asked, could the Christian way of seeing God be reconciled with such a chilly, abstract, remote sort of deity as Aristotle talked about? Christians believed that God was loving, active, at work in the world, concerned with his human children, always ready to help those who asked him. He was perfectly good, not in the abstract sense of Aristotle's "goodness"—as only the fulfillment of potentialities—but in the warm and concrete sense in which Jesus talked about God's "goodness" as the care shown by the loving heavenly Father. The two points of view seemed to be poles apart.

Yet Aristotle's writings were being read by students

and thinkers all over Europe. Unless the readers were very stupid, they could not help being impressed by the accuracy of much of Aristotle's observations, the cogency, or soundness of his reasoning, and the appeal his books made to intelligent minds. Here was a man who did not know the Christian revelation. But here was a man who showed that human reason could—and did—reach obviously compelling conclusions. What was to be done about this very important matter?

Saint Thomas undertook the task of reconciling the two positions. By his distinction between reason and revelation, he made a first step. By his distinction between nature and supernature, he made another. In other words, Thomas tried to show that by reason, such as Aristotle used, it was possible to demonstrate *that* God is and that the world exists only as dependent upon God. If we wish to know *what* God is, in his love, activity, work in the world, concern for his human children, and readiness to answer and help them, then we must turn to revelation and learn about God through faith. That was the point of Thomas' whole effort. Successful or not, for many centuries, once it had been accepted, it provided the way in which most people looked at the relationship between human thinking (or philosophy) and Christian faith.

Some disagreed violently with Thomas, of course, both in his own lifetime and in the years which followed. They thought that he was too confident of the power of human reasoning. They felt that he had worked out altogether too neat a scheme. They believed that he had not taken seriously enough the way in which human willfulness and prejudice interferes with our thinking, twisting and distorting it to serve our own selfish ends. Three centuries later, in the age of the Reformation, men like Martin Luther were especially violent in their attacks on this point, although they often criticized Thomas for what other "scholastic" (medieval) thinkers had actually said. Nonetheless, until quite recently the entire Roman Catholic Church has taken its stand on that system which Saint Thomas developed. He was regarded for centuries in Roman Catholic intellectual circles as *the* theologian; and during the past century, in particular, his teaching has been considered the official teaching of that Church. Today this is not quite so much the case, especially during the last quarter-century and particularly after the famous Second Vatican Council in the 1960's. But Saint Thomas is still to be reckoned with.

To understand Thomas' work more clearly, let us look at one of his modes of arguing. This has to do with what he calls "the five ways" of showing the existence of God. He rejected what was then a popular way of showing God's existence, known as the ontological argument. This argument says that God is to be defined, necessarily, as "that than which nothing greater can be conceived." The human mind simply cannot think of anything greater than God. But suppose that God does not exist? Then we can think of something greater than God. For we can think of God as existing, and that would be greater than a God who did not exist. Therefore, the argument claims, God *must* exist.

This argument, Thomas said, may seem correct, but it is only a matter of words. It does not really prove anything, except that we have certain ideas. It does not show that what we think is actually true. So he rejected the ontological argument—and this was offensive to many, since that argument had been advanced by the saintly and learned Saint Anselm, who, a century before, had been one of the greatest of Christian thinkers, as well as a famous archbishop of Canterbury in England.

Instead, Saint Thomas advanced his own five arguments. First, he said, everybody sees and knows that things in the world are always changing. That is the way things are; there is simply no denying it. Everybody also knows that when there is change, somebody or something must have started it. If we see a ball rolling on the ground, we must assume that it has been thrown or kicked by somebody. Hence, said Thomas, there must be some explanation of change—or motion, he called it, in the usual word of his day. The only reasonable explanation is a "changer" who is not himself subject to change—that is to say, an "Unmoved Mover."

Second, said Saint Thomas, everybody knows that there is a cause, or reason, for what happens. Something causes something else; that something else is called the effect. But the same line of reasoning applies as in the case of change. Somewhere, sometime, somehow, there must be a cause which starts the process of continuing cause and effect. Thus, Thomas argued that the only sensible answer is that there is a "First Cause" who began it all.

Third, everyone knows that in the world everything depends upon everything else—everything is "contingent," not independently itself. This and that and the other thing all hang together in such a way that no one thing could exist without other things. But to make sense of this state of affairs, surely there must be one "necessary" thing, something upon which everything else depends, but which is itself independent of them. And so "Necessary Being" is suggested by the mere fact of a world with contingent, or mutually interdependent, beings.

Fourth, Thomas argued, we all talk about things being better or worse, more or less perfect. And everybody assumes that when we talk in this way we are not talking nonsense. Things actually are better or worse, more or less perfect. But to make any sense out of doing that, we must conclude that we have some kind of awareness that there is a Perfection itself. Otherwise, we could not speak of things as being less than perfect.

Fifth, everyone naturally thinks and acts on the assumption that what he sees in the world has some purpose or reason for existence. There is an ordered arrangement, so that, for example, acorns become oak trees and do not become tigers. There seems to be some sort of "government" in things, with a pattern which is being worked out. But to talk in that way about a particular thing, as we do, implies that there is some principle of government or pattern. For Thomas, that means a "Governor" of the world.

When Saint Thomas concludes each of these lines of argument he says that the conclusion reached is "what men call God." Thus, God is Unmoved Mover, First Cause, Necessary Being, Absolute Perfection, and Supreme Governor. None of these "ways" was entirely new with Saint Thomas. What was new was his fashion of stating them, largely taken from Aristotle, and his putting them together in such a manner that they seemed to add up to a very strong demonstration of God's existence.

However, as we said before, all this can only show *that* God exists. His *character* is known to us through our accepting, by faith, what God reveals to be his innermost nature.

Another interesting part of Saint Thomas' system is his way of answering the difficult question, "How can we use human words, and draw from human experience, to talk about God?" After all, God is far beyond our human minds. He is infinite and he is mysterious. Is it possible for us to speak of him as we do? If so, how?

Thomas' response was that we can use language in three ways. We can use it *univocally,* in which the words we use have an actual identity with what we talk about. So, we say, "the flower is blue"—and so it is. Or we can use language *equivocally,* in which the words are used in an entirely different sense from their common meaning. We say, "I felt blue"—when, of course, we did not really "feel" that we were colored blue at all. The word "blue" is used to indicate a depressed mood, not a color in the spectrum. Finally, we can use words *analogically,* which means that they are used to speak of something which is like, but not the same as, the ordinary sense that the word has. Thus, we say, "God is our father." We are not claiming that God is our father in the way that our male parent is our father, nor do we say that God is entirely unlike our father on earth. What we want to say is that God resembles earthly fathers because he cares for us, loves us, and wants the best things for us, although he does these things in a much higher and perfect way—which Thomas called "in an eminent manner."

Thomas concludes that when we speak about God we always speak in the analogical way. Our words are not adequate, of course, but they are the only ones we possess. And if we are to speak about God at all, this is the way in which we must do it.

There are two other important elements in Thomas' system. The first is what he thought about man himself; the second concerns his teaching about the way in which Christ is present to the faithful in the bread and wine of the Holy Communion, or Mass.

Thomas rejected altogether the notion that a human being is "a soul resident in a body," a popular idea in his time. Taught by his study of Aristotle, as well as by his common sense, Thomas said that man is *both* soul and body. A man without a body would not be a man. On the other hand, a man without a soul or mind would not be human. So Thomas took over from an earlier Christian thinker, Boethius, the view that man is "an individual substance of a rational nature," whose "stuff" is material or bodily, but whose uniqueness is in his capacity for thought. He is not only a body but a soul, and the two are united in him in such a way that he is a "rational animal," unlike angels (souls without bodies) on the one hand or mere animals (bodies without rationality) on the other.

Furthermore, Saint Thomas was able to use for his own purposes Aristotle's notion of "goodness." Aristotle thought that goodness consists in realizing—making actual—the possibilities we possess. Saint Thomas agreed. But he added that the way in which we realize, or make actual, our possibilities is only by obeying the "law of our nature," which is God's purpose for us. As an example, the law of man's nature is that he should live and act as a rational creature, obedient to God's command to live in justice and love with others. Man is supposed to be, and act as, a man. He is not to behave like a monkey or a cat, a

105

snake or a dog. God's command to each man is "Really *be* what you *are*." That is what establishes human dignity, since we are free to become what we were made to be. As the English essayist, G. K. Chesterton, once said, "Only to a man can you meaningfully say, 'Be a man.' You cannot say to a crocodile 'Be a crocodile.' A crocodile is being a crocodile to the limit of his power, but men can *become* more human."

Saint Thomas' teaching about the presence of Jesus Christ in the sacrament of Holy Communion is very important for Roman Catholics, since that teaching is their official doctrine on the subject. According to Thomas, when a priest blesses, or consecrates, the bread and wine used in the sacrament, a real change takes place in those "elements." They remain exactly as they were so far as their appearances go. Their ability to be seen, felt, or tasted is not changed. But their inner reality, their "substance," what they really are in God's eyes, is no longer bread and wine. It is changed into, or converted into, Christ's "spiritual body" and "spiritual blood." By this, Thomas says, he means that *totus Christus,* "the whole Christ," is made present in, and is received by those who take, the communion.

There are many people, of both ordinary and outstanding intellectual powers, who do not feel that the grand system which Saint Thomas Aquinas so carefully and painstakingly built can be accepted any longer. Some other vision of the totality of things must take its place, and there are several possibilities which later great thinkers, both Christian and non-Christian, have offered for consideration. But at the same time, it is difficult not to feel tremendous respect for Saint Thomas' accomplishment. Without doubt, it is one of the most magnificent pieces of intellectual construction known.

Every great effort of the human mind to understand and interpret the "sum of things entire" deserves respectful attention. Modern people are not necessarily any wiser than their ancestors, although they may possess a great deal more information. Truly educated persons must attend to what Saint Thomas wrote; that is the way in which they can pay tribute to his greatness.

It must be said that many Christian thinkers today feel that Thomas' great synthesis fails in one crucial respect. In his effort to bring together the thought of Aristotle, and other Greek philosophers, on the one hand, and the portrayal of God found in the Bible, on the other, Thomas over and over again permits the former to control, or dominate, the latter. Look, critics say, at how Thomas is led to talk about God. He accepts the line taken by non-Christian thinkers and uses phrases for God such as a "being subsisting entirely from itself" or "Unmoved Mover" or "completely fulfilled actuality." All such phrases suggest God as inert, changeless, and unaffected by his world. The sort of God they imply is so much an abstract intellectual construction that it is hard to see how he can be what Christians believe him to be: "pure unbounded love."

On the other hand, there is a second Thomas, who addresses God in hymns and prayers, and speaks about God as the living, active, loving one, to whom his human children may turn and in whom they may put their trust. This is the biblical view of God, and it seems in contradiction to the philosophical one which Thomas adopts. The critics say that Thomas did the best that he could do, for his time and circumstances, but that his synthesis is, in this respect, a magnificent failure even though it is also a magnificent accomplishment.

Thomas has also been criticized for feeling that God's revelation, or disclosure of himself, has been given primarily in "propositions," or statements about himself. This is a different view from the Bible, which talks about God as disclosing himself in what takes place in history or in the lives of men. Once again, they say, Thomas' view is overintellectualized. And they point out another example in the way that Thomas defines faith as an assent to statements about God and about God's nature, rather than (as the Bible says) a courageous commitment of a man's life to God. In that case, intellectual statements about faith would come second to the act of commitment, or trust, itself.

Both Roman Catholic and other Christian thinkers make these criticisms of Aquinas' synthesis of philosophy and faith. His system finds opposition in today's world, where people are so strongly impressed by a changing, evolving, and living picture of how things are. But his system also commands much respect. These two attitudes are not contradictory, since it is possible to respect a man or a position even when not agreeing with either.

Thomas Aquinas was a great man who made a brave attempt at a synthesis of philosophy and faith. If, indeed, he failed in that attempt, it can be said that he was, in one way, like everyone else—a man of his own time.

7.

Controversies and Condemnations

ALTHOUGH Thomas Aquinas was a loyal son of the Catholic Church, he was also an independent thinker. Therefore it was almost inevitable that his teaching would not be accepted at once by all those in positions of academic eminence. And so, within the Church there arose controversies about his views. Some of his opinions were rejected during his lifetime and some after his death. Occasionally, warnings to the faithful about the errors supposedly found in his teaching appeared in official documents. And, of course, there were other controversies, either with actual opponents, such as Siger of Brabant, himself a distinguished philosopher of the time, or with what we might call traditional enemies of Christian teaching, such as the "Gentiles," which at the time meant the group of thinkers who had been influenced by Moorish philosophy, or the advocates of the so-called Manichaean views.

Let us take a brief look at the dissenting opinions of the Platonizing theologians, the radical nominalists, the Moorish interpretation of Aristotle's philosophy, and the Albigensian heresy, based upon a Manichaean theory of the evil of the created world.

For many years the Platonizing theologians' interpretation of Christian faith had been accepted. Very likely they regarded it as the only right way to interpret that faith. Most of the older *magistri,* or theological masters, in the universities shared their view. It was inevitable that when a new approach was proposed, especially by so attractive a lecturer as Thomas, they should feel considerable alarm.

Their point of view seemed to fit the Christian faith quite readily, but the same could not be said about the Aristotelian philosophy, which was cold-blooded, scientific, and purely rational. The Platonizing method allowed for religious experience and, above all, insisted that deep in every man's life there was a genuine contact with God. Aristotle could not easily be read in that way.

Accordingly, one of the first problems that Thomas faced intellectually was to show that Aristotle could be used by a Christian thinker, without any danger to Christian faith. Nobody doubted Thomas' own faith nor his good intentions, but many thought that he was attempting the impossible. When he demolished, as he thought, the famous ontological argument for God's existence, he did so on the grounds that it put too much emphasis on ideas in men's minds, and assumed that those ideas must correspond with how things go in the "real" world. But behind this rejection was Thomas' acceptance of Aristotelian logic, or rules for sound reasoning. Furthermore, he did not think that men "participated," as Anselm and other Platonizers declared, in the very being of God himself.

Thomas was not only in debate with the Platonizing theologians, however. He also had to face the attacks of those who were basically skeptical about religious knowledge altogether. These thinkers did not deny, or at least not publicly, that it was possible to have faith in God, but it was impossible, they said, to have knowledge of God, in the sense in which a philosophical mind wishes to have it.

Such brilliant teachers and thinkers naturally had their supporters. They, too, felt that Thomas used reason in an improper fashion and simply forced it to agree with faith. And they were sure that this could not be done.

Other thinkers strongly emphasized the nominalist position, which said that a word only indicates a number of similar objects. To Thomas, as to all the intellectuals of the time, it was a crucial issue, not just a matter of how words are used. One aspect of the argument concerned how the use of words affected the doctrine of the Trinity, or the Christian doctrine of the threeness-in-oneness of God. A man who believes that words stand for an eternal reality—a realist—will interpret the words "Father, Son, and Spirit" quite differently from the nominalist, who sees words as only convenient human tags for objects in our experience or in our thought.

Furthermore, if nominalism is pushed very far, it can suggest that all human talk about everything is simply a matter of convenience. Our words have no relation at all to how things truly are in the world, but are only human words which have a purely human use. That direction of thought can lead to complete skepticism. It can imply that we never know anything about anything, and that we ought not to claim that our descriptions have any genuine connection with what they are supposed to describe.

Thomas was acutely aware of this danger. He could not accept the idea that there was a sort of eternal realm where everything that our words stand for lives forever. On the other hand, he was certain that to say that human speech has no true reference to things could only lead to intellectual confusion, and finally, to an entirely meaningless world. So, he tried to take the middle path of conceptualism—we only know that there are eternal realities through the actual world of experience, but the words we use to express that experience are truly related to how things are eternally. Hence, Thomas could be, and was sure to be, attacked from both sides. He had to work out his position very carefully and defend it time and time again with arguments to show the error of the complete realists, as well as the error of the very skeptically inclined nominalists.

The interpretation of Aristotle's writings posed still another controversial issue. The Moorish, or Arabian, philosophers had their own interpretation, and it could be made to sound very plausible, indeed. Their interpretation of Aristotle involved complicated technical points, such as whether or not there is individual intelligence which each man has for himself, or whether there is a sort of generalized intellect which everybody shares. If the latter were true, we could not think of John or Mary or Frank as having individualized minds. But to give up that sort of individuality would be to say that there is no such thing as a human personality who is responsible to God for his thoughts, whom God knows as a particular individual, and who counts as such in the world. And there are other consequences, equally serious. At any rate, with such an interpretation, it was entirely impossible to use Aristotle in a Christian philosophy.

Once again Thomas had to face these issues, and he debated them both in his university disputations and also in his writings. Much of his great *Summa contra*

Gentiles is, in fact, directed at the Moorish interpreters of Aristotle. Thomas believed that their interpretation was not only wrong in a Christian sense but also wrong as an interpretation of Aristotle himself.

Finally, Thomas had to face the Manichaean controversy. This was especially important to him, since one of Saint Dominic's purposes in founding the Order of Preachers was to overcome the "Manichaean heresy" as it was expressed in southern France and elsewhere. The Manichaean view was held by the strange sect known as Albigensian, so called because they had originated around the city of Albi in Provence. Because of their energetic preaching, these people had secured a large following, which for many years posed a serious threat to the Christian Church in that part of France and elsewhere in Europe. The Albigensians had a great distrust of the material world, as well as an equally strong distrust of the human body. They thought of the world and of the body as being essentially evil. This idea was a return to an ancient, and for a period widespread, type of thinking in the later days of the Roman Empire. Saint Augustine had once been a Manichaean, as those who held this position were called, after their supposed founder, an eastern sage given the name of Mani. Augustine had finally left the sect, but many others in the early days of the Church either retained Manichaean ideas when they became Christians or strongly opposed Christianity because it held that the world and the body must be good—good

115

because they are God's creation and God does not create anything evil.

It would have been bad enough if the Albigensians had simply opposed Christianity itself. But they also rejected marriage, believed all sexual acts to be evil and dirty, and adopted an entirely negative attitude toward the affairs of organized society. They were a threat to both Church and civil society. Since they rejected marriage, some of them simply had nothing to do with the opposite sex. But others—or so it was said at least—felt that since the flesh was so evil, it could have nothing whatsoever to do with man's real and good life in the Spirit. Therefore, it was perfectly all right to do whatever one wished with the body. Sexual license and immorality would not hurt the soul, which was all that mattered to them.

This movement flourished in many small towns and villages in the countryside, in small groups throughout Provence, and in northern Italy, as well as in other parts of Europe. Albigensian disciples taught their doctrines, greatly disturbing the faithful Christians and the ordinary citizens with whom they came into contact. Thomas undertook to demolish the more theoretical side of the Albigensian position. He knew that it was essential to show how false their basic assumptions were. So, he argued against them on two main grounds.

First, he used reason as an argument, and, second, Holy Scriptures. Neither argument would carry much weight with the Albigensians themselves, but each would be effective in building up a case against their philosophy so far as thoughtful people of the age were concerned. This was important, since there was a certain attractiveness about the simplicity and often obvious sincerity of this sect.

From reason, Thomas could show that there was no sense in condemning the natural world as evil when all men depended upon its fruits and were sustained by the various elements found there. Logically, it could be demonstrated that there is an implicit contradiction in thinking of men as if they were pure spirits whose bodies are irrelevant. From the Bible, Thomas could show that, as Genesis says, God created the world and "saw that it was very good." Hence, it was contrary to the biblical position to see the world as thoroughly bad.

Thomas was prepared to admit the facts of evil in the world and of sin in man. But he argued that evil is a defect in what is essentially good, and that sin is the consequence of free human choice. In neither case can it be said that world and man are evil in their very roots. Whatever evil or sin there is resembles a parasite which can live only so long as the host endures. When the host has died, the parasite dies, too. If evil were as widespread and pervasive as the Manichaean position would claim, then it would long since have succeeded in destroying itself. It can exist only as a contrast to, a negation of, or a distortion in, what is in itself good. In Thomas' own words, *nothing* is evil in and of itself.

117

It is important to observe that in almost everything that Thomas says in opposition to any of the positions against him—whether the Platonizers, the nominalists, the Moorish interpretation of Aristotle, or the Manichaean heresy—he is eminently just to the ideas that he criticizes. He is also honest in facing up to the objections that can be made against views he regards as sound. And throughout his discussions, highly intellectual and precisely logical, is a sense of what might be called a good spirit. His interest is not so much in demolishing people as in changing their minds. He appeals to their reason, to their common sense, and to their own honesty and fairness. All this is typical of the spirit which he himself showed in personal relationships.

Thomas Aquinas did not have what is called *odium theologicum,* which may be translated as "a cantankerous spirit in talking about theology." In a way this infuriated some of his opponents. They wanted to engage in a quarrelsome disputation. Instead, they found that Thomas was reasonable, courteous, fair, and kindly. On the very few occasions when he was not, it was because his opponent's pretentious claims or his use of cheap and shoddy argument seemed a violation of what Thomas believed to be something profoundly human—that is, the capacity to reason and the willingness to follow where reason leads.

During his lifetime, as we have said, there were some strong condemnations of Thomas' teaching. They

118

did not get very far, especially after the Holy See —the papal court and its officials—came out strongly on Thomas' side in many matters. But three years after his death, in 1277, the bishop of Paris, at that time a man called Tempier, included some bits of Thomas' public teaching in an official condemnation. Two hundred and nineteen "errors," said to have been current in the faculty of arts of the University of Paris, were listed. Not all of the errors were from Thomas, but a number were. The senior faculty of theology at Paris, as well as the same group at the University of Oxford in England, disliked much of Thomas' "Aristotelianizing." So also did two successive archbishops of Canterbury in England. One was Robert Kilwardby, himself a Dominican, who was strongly anti-Thomist. The other was John Pecham. They made their denunciations of Thomas between 1277 and 1292.

Pecham was particularly opposed to what he regarded as Thomas' very untraditional portrayal of human nature, which the archbishop denounced as "anti-Christian" in tendency and in conclusion. At the same time Pecham tried to make it clear that he was not intending to attack the Dominican Order or the man Thomas himself, to whom he referred as "a man of holy memory."

However, the criticisms died down, and, in 1319, at a disputation held in Paris, a thesis was put forward and defended which said that "the doctrine" (the

119

systematic teaching) of "Brother Thomas could be taught at Paris with respect to all its conclusions." And in the year 1325, after Thomas had been canonized by the Roman see, Stephen Bourret, then bishop of Paris, made a formal statement in which he revoked the condemnation made by his predecessor in the office, so far as that condemnation "touched or seemed to touch the teaching of blessed Thomas."

Thus, at last Thomas came into his own. Before his death he had the support of the leaders in the Roman *curia* and of many other important theological experts. And not long after his death and the short period of condemnation, he was once again seen as a man who had tried, in all good faith, to commend Christian belief to the intellectual world.

8.

Thomas the Man and the Saint

In his own lifetime, and ever since his death, Thomas Aquinas has been recognized as an intellectual giant. Less than fifty years after he died, the Roman Catholic Church placed his name in the roster of its saints. In doing so, the Church recognized him as more than a great intellectual; it held him as a holy and godly man.

There were many stories told about Thomas after his death, which brought out aspects of his life and personality other than his intellect. These aspects are also important in viewing Thomas Aquinas—man and saint.

As we know, Thomas was a corpulent man. He himself joked about it. Whether or not the stories of his size were exaggerated, he was big. He was also a quiet person, of aristocratic bearing. He could sit for hours reading a book, or sometimes "just thinking." But when he was not in his cell in the monastery or religious house, or in the chapel at one of the many daily services, or at a meal in the refectory, he walked. It is said that he was accustomed to walk around and around the cloister, going very rapidly and almost furiously. If somebody stopped him with a question, as seems often to have happened, he would respond courteously, but then resume his walk.

Thomas was a man of silence, but also a man of good temper. What is more, he was willing to put himself to a good deal of trouble on behalf of other people. One illustration of this is his care in answering the letters that came to him. As Thomas became more and more famous, anybody who had some problem in the philosophical or theological realm felt free to write and ask his advice or opinion. However, letter-writing was not so easy then as now. A busy man in the thirteenth century did not dictate letters to his secretary. If Thomas answered the requests for assistance, he had to do it himself, in his own hand. He seems to have done this very faithfully, for there are records which tell of many cases where people who were strangers to him received answers to questions which were sometimes very silly. As an example, he was asked by someone whether or not the names of all the blessed—those

122

who had died in faith in Christ—were written on a large scroll which was exhibited in heaven. It was a silly question, and nobody would be surprised if Thomas had simply thrown the letter away without reply. But he answered it, briefly but pointedly: "So far as I can see, this is not the case. But probably there is no harm done if somebody says it is so." It was a quiet and gentle answer, with a certain bite to it—"to talk like that is probably harmless, but it is also pointless."

Thomas was taciturn, but, as we know, he had a sense of humor. He enjoyed jokes and even little pranks. When talking about the nature of man, he said that man is not only "a rational animal" but also an *animal risibilis,* "a laughing animal." In discussing how men are to behave, he suggested—quite seriously but probably with a twinkle in his eye—that it is a good thing to vary the earnestness of daily duty with humor and with play.

Because he was essentially a scholar, Thomas valued the things of the mind much more than those which could bring tangible rewards. On one occasion, when he was standing on a hill overlooking Paris, some friends pointed out the great city and one of them remarked, "Wouldn't it be grand to own all this!" To which Thomas replied, "I would rather have that manuscript of Chrysostom that I can't get hold of." He was referring to a book written by one of the great preachers and teachers of the early Church, who had been bishop in Constantinople and was regarded as a noted commentator on the Scriptures. Unfortunately, the book was lost.

As a friar, Thomas could not have many possessions, for one of the vows he took was that he would own nothing for himself. He had been brought up in a wealthy home, but he had renounced all riches. He did not even wish to be a resident dignitary in a great monastic establishment like Monte Cassino, since to occupy such a post would have entailed an interest in those worldly goods. No individual monk could possess such things, but the monastery as an institution could and did. Thomas wanted to be poor; and poor he became, save in the things of the mind.

Things of the mind can be shared. That is why Thomas took trouble to reply to his correspondents. And above all, it explains why he wrote as much as he did. He did not keep his intellectual discoveries to himself, nor did he confine himself to sharing them only with his students. He wrote dozens of essays and many books of considerable length. Among his works was a treatise on the meaning of the Mass, which Thomas had been asked to write when he was teaching in Paris. His fellow theologians gave him the problem of the change in the elements of bread and wine in the sacrament. He wrote a very careful treatise, characteristically lucid and detailed in exposition of his view of the matter. It took a great deal of time and trouble, and when he had finished writing, it is said that he went into the chapel, threw down the manuscript at the foot of the crucifix on the altar, and knelt in prayer. The story says that there were others in the chapel at the time, and they claimed to see a vision. The figure of Christ came down from the cross, stood on the manuscript, and said: "Thomas, you have written well about this sacrament of my body."

Thomas also wrote sermons. A number of them have survived and some may be read in Dr. Martin D'Arcy's selections from Thomas. They are fairly short, very direct, filled with quotations from the Bible, and always concerned with leading his hearers to deeper faith or to the more responsible expression of the Christian life. They are intended to preach the Christian gospel and awaken a response in the hearers.

Among his *explicationes* (brief and fairly popular explanations of well-known Christian formulae) there is one on the Apostles' Creed and another on the Lord's Prayer, but they have not yet been translated into English, with the notes which would help modern readers to understand them. Yet, they are very readable, direct in approach, and uncomplicated. Thomas cites appropriate passages from the Bible, with occasional references to the writings of Saint Augustine.

Thomas was also a poet. He does not seem the sort of person who would have engaged in picturesque and even romantic writing, yet his poems, which are really hymns, are very beautiful. They have many allusions to passages in the Scriptures, giving them a biblical

125

quality. They are very tight compositions, using a minimum of words.

In writing most of his poems, Saint Thomas evidently had in mind the composition of the special services held for the Feast of Corpus Christi. One of the prayers is worth quoting in full, since even in English it is a beautiful composition: "O God, who in this wonderful sacrament hast left unto us a memorial of thy Passion, grant that we may in such wise venerate the mystery of thy Body and Blood, that we may find in ourselves the fruits of thy redemption; who livest and reignest with the Father and the Holy Spirit, God world without end." The prayer is addressed to Christ, believed by all faithful Catholic Christians to be present in the sacrament of the Holy Communion. It expresses simply but without rhetoric the faith which Catholics hold, and prays that what is believed in that faith may produce in those who hold it the "fruits" (the results) in practical living which will show that it is indeed devoutly accepted.

Thomas was a devout Christian who did not like to talk about his inner life as a believer, feeling that this should be a secret relationship between the Lord and himself. Yet there are hints, from time to time, which show the reality and depth of his religious life. Sometimes these are found in an occasional sentence in some very learned and abstract discussion. More often they are contained in stories told by those who knew him well.

For example, just before his death at the monastery of Fossa Nova, Thomas did what every faithful Catholic wishes to do. He made his confession to a priest who was called in to be with him. The priest said afterward that "his confession was like that of a child of five"; it had been so simple and so childlike.

Another story tells of the time when he was praying in the Church of Saint Dominic in Naples. It is said that the crucifix before which he was kneeling had a striking representation of Christ. Thomas was rapt in prayer. The Christ figure on the crucifix spoke to him. Christ said that Thomas had written very well about the Christian faith, and then asked him what he would like as a reward, among all the things which the world has to offer. Obviously, Saint Thomas was not the kind of man who would wish to receive a great kingdom or riches. He might, however, have asked for something in the realm of the intellect, perhaps the solution of some great problem in philosophy or the answer to a theological question. Instead, Thomas answered: "I will have *thyself*."

That answer is interesting, in that it combines the two things that are so notable in Thomas. First, it is very humble, for Thomas asks for nothing tangible, either in the world of material things or in the world of the mind. He wants, as every devout Christian must want, to know his Lord and to know him as well as it is possible for any human creature to do. So there is genuine humility and simple devotion in the reply.

But there is also boldness, almost audacity. For Thomas simply said, "I will have . . ." In other words, that is what I *want*. Indeed, some were so shocked by this boldness that they modified the story a little and have given Thomas' answer as two words, "*Only* thyself," which gives another tone to the reply. But Thomas *was* a bold man; he dared to think about the most profound mysteries of the Christian faith, and he had the courage to look honestly and unflinchingly at the most difficult problems which philosophers can consider.

Another story concerning his innermost life takes place in France, where he engaged in disputation with the famous Siger of Brabant. Siger was a very acute thinker, but he was also a very skeptical man. Thomas had been called to engage with him in public argument, and he had demolished Siger in open debate. In the course of the debate Thomas had said some strong things. "If anyone boastfully takes pride in his supposed wisdom and challenges what we have written about faith and reason, he must not do it in a corner nor before young people who are without power to decide such difficult matters. Let him reply openly if he dare to do so at all. He shall find me there, facing up to him; and he will find not only myself, who does not matter, but many others who study the truth. We shall do battle with his errors or we shall bring a cure to his ignorance."

Thomas spoke like that because Siger's teaching had confused young minds and dismissed those who (like

Thomas himself) tried to reconcile reason and faith. Siger asserted that the followers of Thomas seemed to hold the very double-truth doctrine which he (Siger) presented. This was untrue, but to hint at such a thing was a clever way of making a defense for himself. The incident is one of those very few in which the quiet and gentle Thomas spoke with passion. He was convinced that a great deal was at stake. It was not his own ideas which were being challenged; it was the truth of what he had spent his whole life trying to do. Upon that truth hung the continuing possibility of holding the Christian faith as an intelligible and rational outlook on God, the world, and man.

After the debate with Siger, Thomas returned to Naples. But to the surprise of his close friend, Brother Reginald, Thomas simply stopped writing. He no longer seemed interested in following the controversies that had interested him. He did not complete the *Summa Theologica,* which had engaged his attention at every free moment. Reginald urged him to return to his writing. But Thomas replied, "I can write no more." After a while, Reginald again urged him to continue. This time Thomas said, "I can write no more. I have seen things which make all that I have written seem like straw."

What had Thomas Aquinas seen? It is said that during an earlier celebration of the Mass, he had appeared to be struck dumb. It is generally agreed by those who have studied the record of his last years

129

that Thomas had what is called a "deep religious experience." Whether or not that is true, from that moment on, Thomas wrote nothing. He lived quietly in the Dominican house, carrying on his ordinary duties, engaging much in private prayer, and was always present at the services in the chapel.

Brother Reginald remained Thomas' close friend. Thomas had always had a gift for friendship. He was deeply loyal to his own family, and was especially fond of his sisters. He was also well liked in the religious houses where he lived, and he was certainly devoted to his students, who thronged about him, besieging him with questions and wishing to spend time in his company.

Thomas was also a close friend of the great Franciscan leader, Bonaventura, with whom he went to Rome to plead the cause of the two mendicant orders, the "begging religious"—Franciscans and Dominicans— when they were being attacked by some members of the *curia*. One attack was rather strange, since it came from William of St. Amour, whose book, *The Perils of these Latter Times,* was responsible for the disturbance in Rome. William criticized the two orders because, he said, they were upsetting simple people by their preaching, talking as they did about the love of God and the necessity for thinking hard about the faith. Thomas and Bonaventura were chosen to defend the right of the friars to preach and teach and to move freely about Europe. They were successful in their efforts, and their work together established a very real friendship between them.

Thomas' relationship with Brother Reginald was that of great master to pupil, for Thomas was much older than his friend and confidant. Although Thomas was only about fifty when he died, at that time he was regarded as an old man. People did not live very long then, and men who were only forty years old were often spoken of as "aged." Reginald was probably in his late twenties or early thirties. He was devoted to his master, caring for him in illness, and accompanying him on his last journey north. Thomas evidently leaned heavily upon the love which Reginald held for him. He made no demands upon his younger friend, but he liked to have Reginald with him and he talked to him in a free and confidential fashion.

This dependence on Reginald brings out the very human quality of Thomas' character. He may have been silent and deep in thought much of the time, but he was also a man who loved his fellowmen and enjoyed being with them. Like almost all people, he wanted and needed a close relationship with another person, one whom he could trust and to whom he could talk about the things that were deepest and most real in his own experience.

As a monk, Thomas, of course, did not marry. Although he spent all his life as a celibate, he displayed a healthy attitude toward marriage and the relationships between men and women, especially when he discussed

131

such matters in the second part of the *Summa Theologica*. He did not suffer from the sexual obsession which, it is often said, can be found in such writing by monks. Thomas recognized the place of the body in human experience, and he believed that the body must express itself. He defended and commended marriage as a good, as well as a necessary, state of life. Of course, he urged self-control, and he insisted that sexual relationships should only be enjoyed in the circumstances which he, like all Christian thinkers of his time, regarded as right. But he was not against sex, nor was he a rigorist in his thinking or in his advice.

Saint Thomas had a healthy attitude, not only toward sex and marriage but toward everything else, too. This brought a good deal of criticism from those who thought that he did not delve deeply enough into all the twisted motivations, diseased desires, and the evil in man, or in the world at large. Indeed, it is true that Thomas did not dwell on the evil side of life and of the world, but who is to say that such a fact is to his discredit? Thomas knew that evil was in the world, but he did not think that evil was the main theme in human experience nor in the world as a whole. Thomas' healthy mind was not housed in a healthy body, and throughout his life he knew pain and suffering. He was never in robust health, but was often ill and frequently extremely weary. He worked hard, traveled a good deal, and was continually on call. Perhaps all these responsibilities help to explain his poor health. We do not know the nature of his illnesses, or what caused his death. But in spite of his illnesses, he continued his work, maintaining a sane, balanced, and wholesome way of looking at human beings and at their world.

Thomas Aquinas was a great man, and he was a good man. He was great in body, great in mind, and great in spirit. He was good in soul and heart, in his relationships with others, and in his own devotion to things that in themselves are good. He was a most attractive person.

Some people have been put off by the overwhelmingly academic quality of Thomas' writings, which, except for his sermons, expositions, and poems, are indeed very difficult. They are especially so for people who are not accustomed to such close reasoning and such precise use of terms. A story is told about a woman who decided to read the section of the *Summa Theologica* which deals with "The Simplicity of God." That theological phrase means that God is entirely and utterly *one,* not divided into "parts" or (in the technical term) a "complex being." The woman had thought, from the title, that the material would be very clear and easy to read. But after she had looked through it, she said, "If that is God's *simplicity,* I wonder what his *complexity* must be like!" Of course, she had entirely misunderstood, yet she did have a point.

On the other hand, it is unfair to judge Thomas the man by the inevitable complexity of his writing. It was necessary for him to be very thorough, and to show the greatest precision in the definition and use of terms. But Thomas himself was not a complicated man at all. And it is perhaps easy to understand why this modest and humble, yet intellectually courageous, thinker of the golden period in the Middle Ages has so often won the hearts and minds of those who read about him.

9.

The Influence of Thomas Aquinas

SAINT Thomas Aquinas' great system of thought has sometimes been called "the perennial philosophy." By that, it is meant that his work stands forever as the best and truest account of the whole of things—of God and man and the world and everything else. This is certainly a very strong claim to make, and it would probably be contested by large numbers of thinkers in the world today.

But the phrase "the perennial philosophy" can also be used in another way. It can mean that although the details of his system of thought are not entirely final and unchangeable, his point of view can be called that. If the pattern of things as he described them can be described as "constant," its details are to be filled in as age follows age.

Whether we call Saint Thomas' system "perennial" or not, it has greatly influenced the thinking of man.

Thomas distinguished between the natural and the supernatural. He also distinguished between reason and revelation. Reason is rightly used to learn about nature; revelation is the way in which we can know about "supernature." Reason has to do with the created world; revelation has to do with God. Reason is a human enterprise, engaged in by men; revelation is a disclosure by God, given to men. Reason is the human tool by which we try to know and understand the world. Revelation is a divine gift which we must humbly receive.

Saint Thomas also made another distinction. It is between philosophy and theology. For Thomas, the truth or falsehood of philosophy is determined by how well it stands up to criticism, how satisfactorily it describes and interprets experience, and how self-consistent it is in what it says. But the truth or falsehood of theology (from two Greek terms meaning "words about God") is determined by how well it accepts, describes, and makes sense of that which God has revealed about himself to men. And that indicates a great difference between philosophy and theology.

Yet, Saint Thomas did not wish to make the difference too great. He was convinced that the human mind is able to discover truth, although it cannot discover all truth. And if it can work in this way, it can also arrive at some understanding of God's truth, as well as truth about the world God created. Once again, it cannot understand all God's truth, since God is infinite and mysterious. Yet it is not to be rejected, even before so great a mystery as God. Thomas would have called any such attitude ridiculous, illogical, and possibly blasphemous—because he was sure that God is Truth, in the fullest and deepest sense. To be contemptuous of reason would for him be contempt of God himself.

Understanding this attitude can help us to understand the influence of Saint Thomas in the centuries following his lifetime. His influence has been very considerable, not only in the Roman Catholic Church but elsewhere as well. In any history of human thought, his name has a prominent place.

As we know, Thomas' ideas were by no means generally accepted during his own life. They were regarded as dangerous, and he was often criticized as an innovator who should not be trusted. He seemed too much devoted to Aristotle, some thought. Others said that he was altogether too ready to use his mind on subjects that should be accepted with simple piety and not subjected to critical examination.

Even after Thomas had been canonized in 1323, his opinions were still subject to much criticism. But the censures made in Paris in 1277 were withdrawn, so far as Thomas was concerned. His theological and philosophical system soon became the officially taught position of the Dominican Order. But that still did not mean that everybody then became a Thomist. In the century after his death, there were many who followed Duns Scotus, the great thinker, or Giles of Rome, another philosopher and theologian. And later still, there was another strong school of thought, entirely nominalist in outlook, called after William Ockham. The systems taught by Thomas, Duns Scotus, and Giles were often called the ancient way, which probably meant "old-fashioned thinking." The view taken by Ockham and his followers was called the new or modern way, or up-to-date thinking.

But as the years passed, Thomas' system slowly won its place. Books began to be written about it, just as Thomas himself had written about Lombard's *Sentences.* In the fifteenth century John Capreolus produced a book which brought Thomas' ideas together with those of Lombard's. In the next century, the celebrated Dominican divine Cajetan (his real name was Thomas de Vio, a very famous intellectual of his period) wrote commentaries, or books of exposition, of Saint Thomas' writings. In the same century, Sylvester de Sylvestris produced a large commentary on Thomas' *Summa contra Gentiles.*

In the early seventeenth century, the Jesuit Francis Suarez constructed his *Metaphysical Disputations* on the basis of Thomas' books. In the same period a Dominican writer, John of Saint Thomas, produced a great *Thomist Philosophical Course* (an extended exposition, in great detail) in which he took Thomas' philosophical works and discussed them as separate from Thomas' theological position—although John accepted Thomas' theology as sound and true.

In the eighteenth, and for much of the nineteenth, centuries, Thomas was also highly respected. His theology was now official in the Roman Catholic Church, and among many Catholics his philosophy was also given official status. In 1879 Pope Leo XIII issued an encyclical letter addressed to the whole Roman Catholic Church. In it he said that the philosophy, as well as the theology, of Saint Thomas had "perennial" importance and should be the source of inspiration for all Catholic philosophers and theologians. This encyclical marks the beginning of what today is often known as the Thomist Revival.

The pope did not want people simply to repeat what Thomas had said. He wanted them to know for themselves what he had said, to try to understand it, to see why he had said it, and to find ways in which it might be said again in a new day. Leo's suggestion, coming with the authority of the head of the Church, was very effective. First, Roman Catholic thinkers began to study the actual text of Thomas' writings. Then, led by Cardinal Mercier, the great Belgian prelate who headed the University of Louvain, they began to work through Thomas' views in the light of modern conditions and modern knowledge. As a result, Thomas

Aquinas was born again. He became a thinker who really counted.

But because he was being studied in this way in the Roman Catholic Church it produced consequences outside the Church. This has been due, perhaps, to the books written during the early part of the twentieth century by two of France's most distinguished philosophers, Jacques Maritain and Étienne Gilson. Maritain at one time lectured for several years at Princeton University in the United States; later he was the French ambassador to the Vatican. Gilson taught for many years at Saint Michael's College in the University of Toronto in Canada, and also headed the famous Institute of Medieval Studies at that university. Both men were respected for their work in fields other than philosophy—Maritain in art, social reform, and as a leader of a somewhat left political movement among Roman Catholics in France; and Gilson for his studies in historical aspects of Western thought and also for his work in aesthetics, or the study of the concept of beauty. And they were both Thomists. But there were and are others of the same type. Thinkers outside the Roman Catholic Church respect these men, and through their influence dozens of books written by and about Saint Thomas have been studied by non-Catholics.

This is so much the case that Protestant thinkers today are quite likely to mention Thomas and to quote him just as often as Roman Catholics. And at meetings of philosophers, those who follow Thomas' line of thought are heard with respect. So it is that a man who has been dead for nearly seven hundred years still makes his influence felt.

In itself, such an interest would be confined perhaps to intellectual circles. But because Thomas, in his discussion of the nature of man—to take but one example—is emphatic on the rights due to man as well as on man's responsibilities, following his thought has led recent popes to issue important encyclicals on social justice, the equality of all men in God's sight, and the necessity for looking after their bodies as well as their minds. Two of these papal documents, *Rerum Novarum* and *Quadragesimo Anno,* are responsible for the way in which the Roman Catholic Church has on occasion identified itself with the cause of free, democratic, liberal society, against reactionary or ultraconservative attitudes on social issues. Pope John XXIII, in urging that Christians make common cause with non-Christians in securing for all men decent living conditions, fair play, and just labor-management relations, was speaking from his Thomist background.

Thomas' distinction between "nature" and "supernature" and between "reason" and "revelation" has also had its consequences. Once this distinction was taken with great seriousness in European Roman Catholic circles, a great impetus was given to the study of the world and man through natural sciences. What was discovered in that way would not interfere with

141

religious faith, since the latter belonged (if Thomas was right) in another area. One instance was the foundation of the famous psychological institute at Louvain under Mercier; another was the freedom of inquiry into the physical world, which was taken up by the great French physicist Louis de Broglie.

Furthermore, those who agree with Thomas have felt at liberty to take very seriously some more modern philosophical inquiries, such as the work of the German existentialists and phenomenologists—scholars who describe both what it feels like to be a man and how the world itself looks when it is regarded objectively and simply described in the way that men experience it. Modern Thomists can be open to all these fields of study.

Thus, even today the influence of Saint Thomas Aquinas continues. Many who do not share his particular ideas still regard him as a stimulus to thought. His followers see him as a great inspiration, and think of his books as a guide, as suggestive of the way we can best come to understand our world. When we speak of the influence of a great thinker, it is somewhat different from the influence of a prophetic figure like Saint Paul of Tarsus, who brought Christianity into the non-Jewish world, or of Martin Luther, who is responsible for the Reformation developments in the sixteenth century, with their tremendous consequences for all Protestants. But great thinkers influence the world in more subtle ways, in a less obvious manner. Nonethe-

142

less, they produce great changes in men's minds and provide ideals for men to follow.

Someone has said that while it seems that the world is ruled by force of arms, by military conquest, and by political power, the truth is that the world is really ruled by ideas and by the great men who think those thoughts. If this is the case, then Saint Thomas of Aquinas, who lived some seven hundred years ago in a time very different from our own and who faced problems very different from those modern man must face, has to be taken as one of the rulers of men's minds. Later generations may differ from men like him, but they can never forget them. Thinkers like Saint Thomas are indeed important. We should know about them, appreciate them, and even learn from them, although we must think our own thoughts and come to our own conclusions.

When we look at the great books Aquinas wrote, we seem to be in the presence of two men, not one. On the one hand there is the Thomas who was a devout and intelligent Christian believer; on the other, there was Thomas the expert scholar and exponent of the new ideas which he found in Aristotle. The two Thomases do not always manage to come together, but both are important. The first Thomas has been widely influential because he stated many of the most important points of Christian belief in a clear and straightforward fashion. The second Thomas is important because he sought to work through Aristotle's philosophy and use

143

it for rethinking Christian beliefs. If the second Thomas did not entirely succeed, he still gives us an example of what all Christian thinkers in every age must try to do. Whatever may be the philosophy or way of looking at the world that an age—any age— accepts, such thinkers must work to put the Christian faith in language that takes account of that philosophy or way of looking at the world. And they must do it as honestly and as critically as Thomas himself sought to do, in his own time and place.

Beneath that courteous yet silent manner was a very extraordinary person, a man with a highly acute mind. There was also a profound and humble Christian faith, immense learning, and a thirst to know more. Thomas Aquinas was, indeed, a remarkable man. He had common sense, the hardheaded feeling for reality, and a great trust in the capacity of the human mind to know and to understand. Yet he never allowed himself to step beyond the limits of the human capacity of knowing. He would never claim too much for what he did know. One part of his writing about the existence of God shows this. He asks, "Does God exist?" And he answers at once, "It doesn't look that way." That was a brave recognition of the things that might seem to argue against his own faith. Yet he proceeded to work his way through to the point where he could say, with equal honesty and on the basis of a thorough examination of all the evidence he had, that one could not really doubt that God did exist. If one tried to make sense of the facts which we all know, then he must exist.

Having reached that point, through long, careful, exact, and acute use of his reason, he was prepared to confess that God's character, his active purpose, and his concern for men simply could not be reached in the same way. There was true humility about this acute thinker. At that point he let his own simple faith, learned in childhood and enriched by years of devout prayer and worship, teach him what his inquiries could not discover.

It was appropriate, perhaps, that Thomas should have died where he did, not far from his birthplace, in the land he knew and loved, surrounded by the lovely and rugged Italian countryside, and cared for by Italian monks like those who had taught him as a boy. Thomas Aquinas was Italian in name and in nature, but his influence has gone far beyond his native land, and his name is known and honored wherever men dare to think and to believe.

A Brief Bibliography for Further Reading

Perhaps the reader of this book will wish to continue his study of Thomas Aquinas. There are several books which will help him. The list below includes only the more easily obtainable ones; they are also fairly readable.

Books about Thomas' life:

Chesterton, G. K. *St. Thomas Aquinas.* New York: Sheed & Ward, 1933; Garden City, N.Y.: Doubleday (Image Books), 1936.

This is a simple, straightforward book, which tells a good deal about St. Thomas but a good deal more about how highly Chesterton esteemed his subject. It is not as useful as the two following books.

D'Arcy, Martin. *Thomas Aquinas.* London: Ernest Benn, 1931.

A well-written, sympathetic study by a great scholar. Easy to read.

Selections from St. Thomas' writings:

Thomas Aquinas: Selected Writings, edited by Martin D'Arcy, with an introduction. New York: E. P. Dutton (Everyman's Library), 1934.

St. Thomas Aquinas, Philosophical Texts and *Theological Texts,* edited by Thomas Gilby. New York: Oxford University Press, 1951.

The D'Arcy selection has a number of longer extracts and includes material from St. Thomas' sermons and other writings, as well as from his two great *Summae.* The second pair of "texts" was arranged by Thomas Gilby, also a member of Thomas' own Order of Preachers; the material is in short sections, under the appropriate headings, and is very well arranged and newly translated by the editor. These two books of "texts" are highly recommended.

Books about the thought of the Middle Ages:

Copleston, F. C. *Medieval Philosophy.* London: Methuen, 1952.

A careful and thorough little study, perhaps a little "advanced" for the ordinary reader, but not too difficult. Father Copleston has also written a paperback entitled *Aquinas* [Baltimore, Md.: Penguin Books (Pelican Books), 1955] which is the best single outline of Thomas' thought, but which may be too technical for most readers.

Hawkins, D. J. B. *A Sketch of Medieval Philosophy.* New York: Sheed & Ward, 1945.

A simpler book—also very short and to the point.

Knowles, David. *The Evolution of Medieval Thought.* London: Longmans, Green, 1962.

This is by a historian, not a philosopher or theologian; it is interesting and readable.

148

INDEX